Class Devotions

CLASS DEVOTIONS
for use with the
1992–93
International Lessons

Harold L. Fair

ABINGDON PRESS
Nashville

CLASS DEVOTIONS

Copyright © 1992 by Abingdon Press

ISBN 0-687-08633-7
ISSN 0742-5724

MANUFACTURED IN THE UNITED STATES OF AMERICA

TO MY MOTHER
Clara Williamson Fair
born December 3, 1896
95 years old and going strong!

Preface

As we come into a meeting devoted to the study of the Scriptures and their relevance to life, we must make a transition from the disquiet and cares that have occupied our minds up to that moment to a different world—the world of the spirit. We are coming from a world characterized by spiritual thirst to the well of spiritual water. Jesus told the woman at Jacob's well that "those who drink of the water that I will give them will never be thirty" (John 4:14 NRSV). This living water is the water we seek.

These devotionals are intended to assist in that transition. Each begins with a Scripture reading related to the lesson text and theme for the day. Then follows a brief illustration that invokes the pertinence of the text in a real-life situation. After this illustration comes a brief exposition of the devotional text that relates to both the illustration and the lesson for the day.

Although these devotionals are intended for use in classes studying the International Lesson Series, they can also stand alone and may be used for devotionals of other groups: the women of the church, youth group, other Bible study groups, and the like.

Contents

CONTENTS

READ FROM YOUR BIBLE: GENESIS 13:10-13

At the Crossroads

If we reflect on our past, we too come to intersections often. When we were teenagers, we began to make decisions that affect life today. As life goes on, we come to many crossroads, and, at each one, we make more decisions. As a result, we have come to this present day.

The decisions we have made in the past cannot be reversed. We must live with the results. Our reflection on these decisions may cause us some anguish if we wish we had chosen differently. But alas! The past cannot be altered.

Here are only some typical crossroads we face in life: the decision on whether to study hard in school; the choice of a career; the choice of our lifetime's work; the choice of a husband or wife; the choices regarding whether to have children; choices of where to live; choices of the church to go to and how active we will be; choices of friends; choices of how to raise the children we may have had; choices of how to get along with neighbors or co-workers or fellow church members; choices regarding aging parents; choices regarding local, state, and national politics—these are typical of the decisions many of us make in a lifetime.

If we look back over all the decisions we have made, we see that when we made a choice, life moved in a certain direction thereafter; if we had made a different choice, life would have moved in a different direction.

If we have been unusually wise, when we look back over life, we can say honestly that we would not change a single decision we have made. But most of us wish that we had, in at least one or two crossroads, made a different decision. If we have been fortunate, however, all our decisions have in the end turned out to be satisfactory. Overall, we feel good because we have made as many good decisions.

11

As we read the Bible, we find that the persons whose lives are described there are similar to ourselves regarding decisions they have made.

The previous chapter of Genesis tells how Abram and his ancestors had come to Canaan after hearing God's call. Abram could have refused to obey that call. As a result, he might have lived out his life in the land of his ancestors, and he would never have become the patriarch of the Hebrew nation. During his lifetime, he faced many other decisions that would have momentous consequences for the history of Israel.

In the episode we have read today, Abram and Lot, whose herdsmen had been quarreling, decided that they should go separate ways. Abram gave his nephew the choice of whether to go left or right. The text seems to suggest clearly that Lot's choice—to go to the Jordan River valley and to settle near Sodom—was a faulty one, because he chose to live among people who were sinning against the Lord.

Later Lot was among those captured in a war. Although Abram, his uncle, rescued him, the reader is left with the impression that Lot never again had the stature that he had enjoyed previously. The decision to live near Sodom cast a blight over the rest of his life.

During our adult life, we make many vital decisions. None is more important than the response we make to the call of God. If we make decisions based on selfishness, as Lot did, we may regret it. On the other hand, if we follow the model of Abram and think always of how our decision will reflect on the life of faith, we may be assured that later, when we think about the crossroads to which we have come, at least in our commitment to God, we have made a decision we will never regret.

Let us pray.

Eternal God, as we reflect on the decisions we have made throughout life, we are aware that our motives have not always been the best. We, like Lot, have sought to get the best for ourselves without true regard for the needs and wishes of others. Help us, we pray, as we come to the future crossroads of life, to make decisions that will reflect our commitment to you. We ask this in the name of Jesus. Amen.

READ FROM YOUR BIBLE: EXODUS 4:10-16

Let Someone Else Do It!

Just over three hundred years ago, on September 12, 1687, John Alden died. He was the last of the Mayflower Pilgrims to perish. A hundred and one people had arrived on the Mayflower in 1620, and when John Alden died, there were no others who had come across the Atlantic in that frail craft.

John Alden is best remembered because of a poem written nearly two hundred years after his death, "The Courtship of Miles Standish" by Henry Wadsworth Longfellow. In this poem, Miles Standish, a military commander of the Pilgrims, wanted to ask Priscilla Alden, a young widow, to marry him, but he was too shy to propose, so he asked his friend John Alden to go to Priscilla and deliver the proposal. After Alden had done so, according to Longfellow's poem, Priscilla said to him, "Why don't you speak for yourself, John?" Whereupon, he did, she accepted, and Priscilla and John Alden were married.

Garrison Keillor, the popular host of a public radio variety program, often speaks about his own shyness. Though he appears before thousands of people each week, he has said that he gets painful attacks of anxiety because he doesn't feel confident of his ability, even though he has been on radio for many years.

A popular country music star stutters very badly when he speaks. On Johnny Carson's show, he has told about how miserable his childhood was because other children made fun of him. But he made a great discovery—when he sings, he doesn't stutter. So what he thought was his biggest handicap turned out to be the path to an extraordinary career. He has overcome his shyness because of his speech problem so that he can now talk about it publicly in a humorous manner.

* * *
** ** **

In the passage we have heard today, God informs Moses that he is to go to the pharaoh and bring the Israelites out of Egypt (Exodus 3:10). For the remainder of chapter 3 and into chapter 4, Moses offers up excuse after excuse as to why he cannot perform this task. Later, God agrees that Moses' brother, Aaron, would be the spokesman because he can speak well.

Sometimes we get the idea that people in the Bible were perfect, or at least a lot better than we are. But here we see Moses putting up the same excuses we often make.

How often have we been approached by someone to carry out some task for God, but, like Moses, we have been filled with excuses? Sometimes when we are asked, before we can answer we go into a panic and search urgently for some acceptable reason why we cannot do what we have been asked.

Many—maybe most—of us are shy. We don't want to get up in public or call attention to ourselves. If we had to trust only in our own resources, perhaps we would be justified in saying, "Ask someone else to do it." But God offers us the same help that he offered Moses. He told Moses that he would be there to help, in this case, to provide the words that should be spoken to the pharaoh.

We know from the narrative that follows that Moses and Aaron were able to speak on God's behalf to the Egyptian ruler and that eventually they led the Hebrew slaves out of captivity.

If God calls us to a particular task, he is going to provide assistance for us to accomplish it. We are never alone when we undertake some assignment to God's people.

As we become more practiced, we shall learn, like John Alden, to speak for ourselves, and what began as a handicap may become the best way we can serve God and his people.

Let us pray.

God of all strength, you know when we lack confidence in ourselves, when the extent of our mission seems to be too heavy to bear. But we claim the promise that was made to Moses long ago, that if we undertake a responsibility in your name, you will be with us to provide the help we need to accomplish it. Forgive us when we cry out, "Let someone else do it," and give us courage to follow your call. We ask this in the name of Jesus. Amen.

READ FROM YOUR BIBLE: JOSHUA 3:1-7

Be Ready for Tomorrow

In the year 1838, Frederick Douglass was a slave who lived in Baltimore. He earned six dollars a week, and his master took all his money except six cents.

Since most slave owners wanted to profit as much as possible from their slaves, Douglass proposed to his master that he be allowed to hire out as a day worker. To do so, he agreed to pay his owner six dollars every Saturday with the chance that he might some weeks make more than six dollars. If he did, he could keep everything over this amount.

His master agreed, and Douglass had to work night and day in order to come up with the six dollars. One Saturday night he went to a camp meeting, intending to give the six dollars to the master the following day. Because he did not pay his owner on Saturday, as they had agreed, his owner became so angry that he once again took away Frederick Douglass's freedom to hire himself out.

At that point, Douglass decided to escape from slavery. He developed a specific plan to leave Baltimore and slavery behind and to go north to a state where slavery was not legal. He saved a little money and, after careful planning, made his escape to New York, where he was befriended and protected by white people who opposed slavery.

In the years afterward, when he told this story, he emphasized that his mental preparation had come first. He could not bear the idea of living as a slave for the rest of his life, so he had learned to read and write and he had learned a trade so he could support himself as a free man. Once he made the decision to escape from slavery, he again planned carefully the exact day he would flee and where he would go. Every effort of every day was pointed in the direction of freedom.

When the day came, he was ready to cast off slavery forever and start life anew as a free man. Even today, the personal narrative of his flight to freedom thrills the reader with its demonstrations of intensity and courage.

Like all great leaders, Joshua was a man who planned carefully. The passage we have heard today describes the details of the crossing of the Jordan River as the Hebrews prepared for the conquest of the Promised Land. First, they went to the edge of the river, but they did not cross over. Then Joshua sent officers throughout the camp to give orders to the people. He provided instructions to the priests to carry the ark of the covenant ahead of the people, as the ark was the symbol of God's presence with them.

As the following verses show, Joshua was indeed a fitting successor of Moses. As planned, the Hebrews crossed the river and began to take the land, which even today is claimed by the descendants of those who forded the Jordan on that crucial day more than three thousand years ago.

Frederick Douglass was prepared when the opportunity came for him to escape slavery, just as Joshua was prepared long before his time of leadership actually came, following the death of Moses.

Many ventures in the church fail because of the unwillingness to do careful and thoughtful planning well in advance. Success is not attained because we lack the prior commitment to achieve our objectives. Because we fail to plan adequately, we are stymied by the first difficulties we encounter.

Joshua and the Hebrew people had a promise and a vision of the new land. They were forewarned that hardships would befall them. But they looked beyond the adversities and imagined the time of triumph.

We, like Joshua and Frederick Douglass, must plan carefully to ensure the success of every venture we undertake for the sake of Christ.

Let us pray.

O God, the strength of all who put their trust in you, may we, like Joshua, prepare steadfastly for every task we undertake in your name. Keep us faithful in our endeavors, that we may always be ready for tomorrow. We ask this in the name of Jesus. Amen.

READ FROM YOUR BIBLE: JUDGES 6:11-16

Empowered to Serve

Do the stars foretell the future? In thousands of newspapers and magazines in the United States and elsewhere, daily horoscopes appear. Some people read these "forecasts," and some may even believe that what they find there is the sound basis for planning their lives.

In a book published a few years ago about President Reagan, the author, who had been a member of the government and had worked closely with the Reagans, said that Mrs. Reagan had often telephoned an astrologer in California—someone who claims that the stars and planets foretell the future—to get advice on the president's schedule.

Can a Christian believe that the stars foretell the future? Not according to one of the early saints of the church, Augustine.

During Augustine's time, about three hundred years after the life of Christ, many people believed that the stars foretold the future. Augustine himself imagined that such a belief was pagan, but he could not shake the feeling that perhaps the stars *did* tell about the future.

An event occurred that helped him make up his mind. If two people were born on the same day and at the same hour, according to astrology their lives would be identical. Augustine read an account of two women who had given birth to babies at the same minute on the same day. One mother was a slave, and the other mother was of the ruling class. If the astrologers were right, the two babies should have lived identical lives. But in fact, the son of the slave mother was a slave all his life, while the son of the upper-class mother was a member of that class all his days. When Augustine learned of these consequences, he knew then that human destiny was not ruled by the stars and that the stars did not foretell human events.

* * *
** ** **

The theme of the book of Judges is that, from time to time, righteous leaders were raised up to save Israel from their troubles. These leaders were chosen by God and given the power to do what was needed.

In the episode we have heard today, Gideon was threshing wheat when he received his call to lead the fight against the Midianites, who were invading the land. Like Moses, he protested that he lacked the power to lead, but the Lord responded that he would be with Gideon. In other words, God would provide the power through Gideon. The reading of the following chapters discloses that Gideon and a small number of Israelites were successful in overwhelming the Midianites.

What is the relevance of this experience in the book of Judges to the lives of Christian people? One message certainly is that in a mysterious way God provides the power through us to do what must be done. Exactly how this power is transmitted defies the understanding and the imagination. Yet we know that events do occur that cannot be explained fully in terms of the human effort that goes into them.

One thing is certain: The Bible teaches that astrology is not compatible with Christian belief. No person can believe that God is the provident ruler of the universe and that the stars are also. God does not forecast events through the stars.

Therefore, when Mrs. Reagan was calling on an astrologer to advise her on the president's schedule, she was relying on a pagan belief, not on a Christian belief. God is also the God of the stars, and nowhere in the New Testament do we find affirmed any idea that God's means of revelation is through the heavenly bodies.

We must instead rely on the guidance of the Scriptures, through prayer, and through the counsel of spiritual leaders who can help us discover God's will for us.

Let us pray.

Stir up your power, O God, as in the days of Gideon and the judges of Israel, in order that we may know that the Spirit, through the Scriptures, is the means by which you convey to us your will. May we put away all belief in pagan practices, like astrology, that devalue your providential care over the world you have made. We ask this in the name of Jesus. Amen.

READ FROM YOUR BIBLE: I SAMUEL 8:10-18

God Will Not Answer

An elderly man moved from a rural community where he had lived all of his life to the city because he wanted to be near his only child and his grandchildren.

Before he left his life-long home, he gave his telephone number to all his friends and asked them to call him when they came to the city for any reason. He knew that many of them had family members in the city, that some went to medical specialists there, and that others came to the city to visit the various shopping centers.

He expected that almost from the beginning he would receive some telephone calls each week, and he looked forward to staying in contact with his life-long friends through these calls. After he moved, day by day he sat near the telephone, expecting it to ring and to hear the voice of someone he had known for many years. How disappointed he was when, after several weeks, he had received not a single call.

After three months, he returned to his former home community for a visit, and when he went to church that Sunday, he asked his friends whether they had been to the city. Yes, several of them had. And why hadn't they called him? Several persons said they had tried, but that the telephone number he had given them was apparently not correct. After they had tried to call him, each one had returned home thinking that they had copied the wrong number, but, as it turned out, the man had given his friends the incorrect number. Each time, the telephone had rung many times, but no one had answered.

The passage we have heard today describes a situation in Israel that is readily understandable to us. The people there wanted a king so they could be like other nations.

How often our strongest reason for wanting a change is to be like others. Ads in magazines and on television play toward our feelings of wanting to be like others. We see others having a wonderful time using some product or service, and we want to have a wonderful time too. Often we don't realize until afterward that possession of that object does not automatically bring us the joy we perceived in the advertisement.

When the Israelites became persistent in their desire for a king, the Lord authorized Samuel to fulfill their wish. Before he did so, Samuel warned the people of the consequences of their decision. He informed them that when they became unhappy with their decision, they would cry out to God, but that he would not hear them.

We are human, so we do not like to take responsibility for our decisions, especially if the results are unpleasant. We want to make the decision, but if the consequences are not agreeable, we want someone else to save us. When a child overeats and becomes sick, the parent will usually admonish the child and say, in effect, "You brought this on yourself. Next time, you will know better."

Adults often follow the same pattern as an impulsive child—except with one big difference. A child is only learning, but as adults, we should know when the repercussion of our behavior is likely to be unpleasant.

The advice of this passage is to look forward to the consequences *before* the action is taken. The Christian who violates the moral law will surely pay for the consequences. When we violate the moral law knowingly, it is foolish to expect that God will bail us out, so to speak. We willingly committed the acts. Therefore, we must accept whatever follows.

In the days after Israel received a king, the people had many occasions to regret their choice. But they had to live with the result of their demands. So will we.

Let us pray.

Grant, we pray, Almighty God, that we shall be mature enough to know that if we commit an intentional wrong, we must deal with the results, however disagreeable and unpleasant they may be. Give us the maturity of spirit that will keep us always faithful to your will. We ask this in the name of Jesus. Amen.

OCTOBER 11, 1992

READ FROM YOUR BIBLE: I SAMUEL 16:14-23

Where No One Had Gone Before

Tomorrow, October 12, is a special day for millions of people. Five hundred years ago on that date Christopher Columbus discovered the Western Hemisphere.

Columbus was not easily discouraged. He was a well-trained seaman who was certain that, based on knowledge available at that time, a route to the Far East could be found by sailing west from Europe. He prepared himself for his voyage of discovery through his excellent knowledge of maps and charts, and by sailing on many ships as a crew member in the eastern Atlantic Ocean.

Another important part of his preparation was his study of prevailing winds and sea currents. One remarkable result of his discovery voyage was that he learned how to sail to the New World against these winds and currents. Before Columbus, no navigator had learned this skill.

As the world knows, he set out in tiny ships. He led his crew to believe that the voyage would be short, and as it lengthened to more than a month, they became increasingly uneasy. More than once the crew thought of throwing him overboard so they could return home. But Columbus reminded them, first, of the great treasures he expected to find and that he would share with them and, second, of the dreadful fate that awaited the crew if they returned home without him.

* * *
** ** **

Our reading for today describes how David was invited to serve King Saul. The king knew that he had fallen from God's

22

favor, and he developed what we might call today a persecution complex. In the Bible, this mental and spiritual problem is expressed by the belief that an evil spirit had come upon Saul. His attendants, unusually wise for their time, believed that soothing music would help calm Saul's disturbed mind. David, who had not yet been publicly declared to be Saul's successor, was invited by Saul's attendants to play the harp for Saul. In our time, researchers have proven that soothing music can often help persons who are mentally disturbed, and this therapy helped in Saul's case.

David put his life in peril by coming to Saul's court, because the attendants surely told him of the king's rage from time to time. David, however, was willing to use his skill in music as a means of helping a sick man. In doing so, as far as we know in the Bible, he was the first to use this gift of music for the benefit of another person. He accepted a remarkable risk when he agreed to play the harp for Saul, as he later found out when the king became angry with him.

Columbus also used his skills and gifts for the betterment of untold generations who would follow him. He took risks because he believed in his goal—to find a shorter way to the Far East. He put his own life at risk many times to achieve this goal.

David and Columbus went where no one had gone before.

Risk-taking is not comfortable. The outcome may be uncertain. Yet, as disciples of Jesus, we should follow his example of boldly putting our gifts into service for others, even though we risk being criticized for it.

Persons who "play it safe" never achieve their full potential. If David had played it safe when Saul's attendants asked him to play the harp for the sick king, he would have said, "No thanks. I don't want to be killed by a mad ruler."

If Columbus had "played it safe," he would never have discovered this New World in which we live. He might have died an idle dreamer, but he took risks and so became a person whose place in history is without question.

What risks should we be taking to follow in the footsteps of Jesus?

Let us pray.

Set us free, O God, from our slavery to security, and help us to be unsparing in our determination to follow your example, to risk criticism and reproach for the greater good of serving your kingdom. We ask this in the name of Jesus. Amen.

OCTOBER 18, 1992

READ FROM YOUR BIBLE: I KINGS 11:34-39

A King Who Stumbled

An unusual institution in our society is what has become known as "the crisis line" or "the hotline." These are usually 1-800 numbers that persons can call when they need help but don't know where to turn.

You may have noticed such telephone numbers on your television screen as a part of a news program or a program dealing with a particular personal or social problem. They invite anyone to call who has a problem. At the other end of the line, a person will answer and will listen to the caller's problem in a sympathetic way. If asked, the person may suggest other resources that could help the caller.

National helplines are available on many topics: AIDS, air travel, Alzheimer's disease, alcoholism and drug abuse, arthritis, asthma and allergies, autism, blindness, cancer, child abuse, depression (including suicidal thoughts), diabetes, domestic violence, Down Syndrome, dyslexia (a reading disorder), eating disorders, epilepsy, head injuries, hearing problems, heart disease, hospices, impotence, kidney disease, learning disabilities, and lung disease, just to name a few.

Many public libraries have available listings of many of these helplines. Any individual may call these numbers to discuss a problem. Sometimes individuals need general information; sometimes they need to talk to someone who has had experience with the same problem. These helplines can provide assistance on most questions like this.

The best part is that calls to these helplines are usually free and so is the advice you get from the person you talk to. Many people are desperate for support and have no idea where to get relief. Often these helplines are the answer to a prayer. For instance, you may have a family member who has Parkinson's disease and you want to know how to help this person. You could call the Parkinson's Educational Program's 1-800 number, which is answered around the clock, twenty-four hours a day.

In the account we have heard today, we learned something that Solomon, as wise as he was, did not know—that his kingdom would be split and most of it given to another family after his death.

During his lifetime, Solomon faced many adversaries. Twice God warned him that he should not sacrifice to other gods, but he did not keep the Lord's command. Therefore, he faced the consequences. He must have had many periods of anxiety and depression, for he knew he had disobeyed God. There was no 1-800 number for him to call.

As the story is told in the passage we heard today, his disobedience finally cost his family the kingship of Israel. For the sake of David, Solomon's father, the Lord announced his intention to leave Solomon's family two of the twelve tribes. He would give the other ten tribes to another family after Solomon died.

As God worked through the prophets who advised these national leaders in the Old Testament, he sometimes works today through human channels. These helplines can be the answer to prayer when they offer a desperate individual or family the help they need.

Prevention is better than a cure, however. If Solomon had lived according to his promises to God, his family would have retained the throne of Israel. If individuals today lived by the moral law, many helplines would not be needed, for we bring many disasters upon ourselves.

Forgiveness and help are available, but they must be sought. They do not fall from the sky automatically.

Like King Solomon, we too may stumble. He did not ask for help; therefore, he received none. If we need help, we too must ask.

Let us pray.

Pour your grace into our hearts, O Lord, that we may seek help while it may be found. But let us also remember that penitence is required if we are to have your forgiveness and restoration. May we subdue our pride when we have done wrong, and help us to admit that we have offended you. When we stumble, we shall not fall if we rely on you. We ask this in Jesus' name. Amen.

OCTOBER 25, 1992
READ FROM YOUR BIBLE: II CHRONICLES 34:9-13

They Did Their Work Faithfully

Some of you can remember that a few years ago anything that had on it the label "Made in Japan" was thought to be poorly made. Also, anything that had on it "Made in the United States" signified that its quality was the finest.

Since the rebuilding of Japan following its defeat in World War II, however, almost the opposite statements have become true. Today, Americans seem to believe that any article made in Japan—such as a videotape recorder, a television set, or a car—is of the highest quality. But if the object is made in this country, it is thought to be inferior.

What has happened to cause this shift in attitude? Japanese society is fundamentally different from ours, experts say. Many Japanese put the company they work for ahead of almost all other values, even their families. In this country, management and the work force are often at odds, because each wants more control of decisions and more benefits than the other. Both managers and workers have often forgotten that there is a third party to all their decisions. This third party is the public who buys what the companies produce. If both managers and workers insist that their benefits have priority over everything else, the products may suffer in quality. Managers try to gain by making greater profits, and sometimes this means cheaper, lower quality raw materials, machinery, and processes. The workers try to gain higher benefits by reducing demands of productivity and improving working conditions, but they neglect to insist on quality.

Because of the competition from the Far East, more companies today, including both the managers and the work force, have returned to the stress on consumer values—high quality in the product or service.

At the time Josiah became king of Judah, the worship of God had declined to the point that the temple had fallen into ruin and badly needed repairs. In the passage we have read today, the high priest received money to purchase materials and to pay workmen to renovate the building. The restoration was so flawless that the writer added the sentence, "The people did the work faithfully" (II Chronicles 34:12).

Faithfulness to the task is a special quality. To be faithful means to be trustworthy and dependable in whatever work we undertake. It means that we will be diligent in producing the best possible results under the circumstances.

A worker helping to build the wing of a big airplane took a lot of trouble to be precise in riveting his part of the assembly, though it was hidden from sight. A fellow worker told him that he did not need to be so particular, that no one would know the difference. The worker's response was "I will know."

A theologian once said that the test of a person's religion was what he or she did when no one was watching. Faithfulness means to act with honesty, even when no one else can see what we are doing.

Sometimes in the church we do not make the same effort we make in our public job or work at home. We want our refrigerators and television sets to function flawlessly for years and years—and we expect them to continue working. If they don't, we complain. But in the church, we sometimes give the Lord a feeble effort. One reason we do not see better results in the work undertaken by the church is that people withhold their best.

If we are to be true followers of Jesus, we must do our work faithfully as he did and not try to just "get by" with the least possible devotion. Let us instead be like the laborers who renovated the temple in the time of Josiah and do our work faithfully.

Let us pray.

Purify our conscience, O Lord, that we may shun low quality in our church life. Give us vigor in all things that we undertake in your name, that we may at the end receive the commendation of a faithful servant. We ask this in the name of Jesus. Amen.

READ FROM YOUR BIBLE: I KINGS 19:10-13

Zealous for the Lord

Just before World War I a young man took a walking tour that led him through a barren area in eastern France. For miles and miles, there were no trees, no streams, and no people. He ran out of water, and he was lucky to find a shepherd's cottage in the forsaken district.

The shepherd, who lived alone with his sheep and his dog for companions, told him he could spend the night if he wished. The young man accepted the invitation.

After supper that night, the shepherd put a bucket of acorns on the table. He sorted through the acorns carefully, and he discarded all those that were cracked or had a blemish of any kind.

The shepherd was not a talkative man, and his guest decided that he should not ask the man what he intended to do with the acorns. The next morning, the shepherd took his sheep out to pasture as usual, and the young man followed at a respectful distance. The older man left his sheep in the care of his dog, and, taking his bag of acorns, he began to walk along a treeless hillside. He stopped, and, using a pointed iron rod he carried, he made a hole, dropped in an acorn, and carefully covered it. He walked a short distance farther and planted another acorn in the same way.

He noticed the younger man watching him from a distance, and the shepherd asked his guest to join him. By way of explanation, he said that he intended to plant acorns every day, so that some day the barren hills might be covered with oak trees.

The following day, the young walker resumed his journey. Soon World War I broke out, and he was called into service as a soldier. Luckily, he survived the war. After peace came, he wanted some time to reflect on his future life, so he decided to visit the old shepherd who had planted the acorns.

When he got to the area, he hardly recognized it. He found the shepherd in his cottage. Yes, he had continued to plant acorns during the war, and he had now planted over a hundred thousand. Of that number, ten thousand trees were growing. He took the younger man out to see for himself. His guest was amazed as he saw the acres and acres of small trees.

He left, but after many years, he decided to return again to see the shepherd. When he arrived in the area, he scarcely recognized it. Now the hills were covered with big oak trees; streams that formerly had been dry now flowed with water. Villages had been established. The whole land had been remade. He finally found the shepherd. He was in his eighties, and he told his younger friend that he had continued to plant trees through the years. The whole province had been transformed, all because of one man—who planted trees as his gift to the future.

*   *   *
** ** **

From a human point of view, Elijah's fear for his life is understandable. He fled from those who might try to kill him. When God met him in a gentle whisper, and when he heard a voice ask him what he was doing at Mount Horeb, Elijah declared that he was zealous for the Lord. To be zealous means to be aggressive, hard-working, militant, and energetic.

Elijah offers Christians a good model. Too often we are timid, hesitant, unconcerned, and reserved.

The old French shepherd had a mission in life—to leave the formerly barren hills of his region covered with oak trees. The task seems too great for one person. Elijah must also have thought that his commission was too great. Yet he was zealous for the work of the Lord. We, too, must be like him.

Let us pray.

Heavenly Father, shepherd of your people, often we are timid, hesitant, indifferent, and reserved when we should be zealous for you—aggressive, hard-working, militant, and energetic. In Jesus, we see one who gave us a model. May we be more like him. We ask this in his name. Amen.

READ FROM YOUR BIBLE: AMOS 5:11-15

Hate Evil, Love Good

A few years ago, Poland escaped from the oppression of communism and entered the family of nations as a democracy. For more than half a century, the nation suffered through war, and then became a victim of the domination of the Soviet Union.

In recent times, the situation has improved, at least politically. Yet Poland faces some dark days ahead in dealing with the problems of its people.

Recently, during the summer months, the fields of Poland were white with the blooms of poppies. The pods of these flowers provide the raw materials for morphine, which is used in hospitals and pharmacies.

These poppies produce another harvest, however—darker and more tragic. Thousands of Poles drive into the country when the poppies are in bloom, pluck the blossoms, and cook them to produce a drug like heroine. Thousands of Polish young people have become addicts to this cheap drug.

One dangerous outcome of this drug use is that thousands of these youths are contracting AIDS through infected needles used to inject their homemade drugs.

Officials of the government estimate that the drug epidemic among these young people is going to be far worse than it is in this country. Since Poland is still a poor country, these thousands of persons will die with no hope of treatment.

When Amos was a prophet, no drugs were in use, but the wealthy people of the country were intoxicated with their riches. They lacked compassion for the poor, who lived in the most desperate circumstances.

In a sense, Amos gave a different emphasis to his prophecies than those who preceded him. The priests and the people had grown cold and heartless in their practice of religion. They were convinced that since they went through the prescribed ceremonies, they were meeting their religious obligation.

Amos, however, disputed that attitude. He rebuked the people for their greedy spirit, for their injustice, and for their total neglect of the spirit of the law. God's chosen people, therefore, would pay a heavy price for their indifference—their nation would be overthrown by a pagan nation. This disaster would be the penalty for their lack of compassion toward the poor.

In Poland, the use of drugs is destroying the lives of thousands of young people. They have been warned of the price they will pay, but they pay no attention to the warnings.

How terrible, we think. Yet here in our own nation, the use of cocaine is destroying not only those who use it but our entire society as well. The need for drugs is creating a crime wave that seems to have no limits. We try to stop countries in South America from producing cocaine, but the authorities say that since people in this country buy drugs, someone will produce them. The market must be reduced to stop the import of drugs.

This nation has prophets like Amos. Every community has men and women who try to uphold the commitment to a moral life, but they are often in a minority.

Will this nation have to suffer as Israel did for our loss of righteousness?

Let us pray.

O Lord, you have taught us that the way to virtue is in commitment to your way. We seem powerless to change our society in its headlong pursuit of forbidden pleasures. Yet we dare not give up hope. May we continue our commitment to follow the way of Christ, and to pray that

our nation will awaken before it is destroyed by the millions who seek
well-being through drugs. We ask this in the name of Jesus. Amen.

READ FROM YOUR BIBLE: HOSEA 2:21-23

You Are Mine

The scene in the courtroom is repeated hundreds, possibly thousands, of times each year with a few variations.

A husband and wife in their late thirties watched the jury file back into the room. Their hearts were pounding so loudly they thought everyone in room could hear the beats. A few feet in front of them sat their son, only seventeen years old but on trial as an adult—for murder. He had broken into a neighbor's house while the man was away, but he returned to find the boy taking his television set out the back door. The man called to the boy to put down the television, and he did. But then the boy drew out a pistol and shot the man. He died before the ambulance got there.

Now the parents were waiting for the jury's verdict. Through many sleepless nights the parents had talked and cried, wondering where they had gone wrong in bringing the boy up. The neighbor he had killed was a friend of theirs, had gone to the same church. They agonized in church every Sunday as the widow came in and took her place alone.

Yet they still loved their son, in spite of the terrible crime he committed. In those late-night sessions when the boy was in jail, they got out the picture albums and looked at the photos of him as a baby, taking his first steps, playing in the backyard wading pool, opening his Christmas presents, looking wide-eyed at the candles on his birthday cake. How had this son, on whom they had showered so much love, gone wrong?

Now they waited. How slowly the moments passed as the

jury members took their seats. The parents felt sick with worry. The foreman was asked the question by the judge. His answer: Guilty.

The parents had expected it, but when they heard the words, they were dismayed. Even if he received the minimum sentence, this boy, who seemed to them still only a child, would have gray hair when he left prison. Imagine the loss. The widow had already left the courtroom. Imagine her loss, too.

The boy was taken away to jail before the heartbroken parents could speak to him. He had done wrong, and society said he must pay. The parents had no quarrel with the verdict. As he passed through the door with police officers on each side of him, his mother whispered the words, "You are still mine."

Many families today experience such heartbreak as these parents. Parents go wrong; children go wrong. The result is tragedy that defies description. There are many wounded hearts in this community because someone has made a mistake in judgment and is now having to pay for it. Oh, how deep the agony can be!

The passage we have read today depicts God as the husband of a faithless wife, Israel. The wife has done wrong, but the husband loves her in spite of her wrongdoing.

How can a parent love a child who has done wrong? Or how can a child love a parent who has done wrong? In theory, such questions seem to have easy answers. But to the person who goes through the experience, the sorrow over wasted opportunities and wrong choices is what brings the tears.

Israel made countless choices against God's morality. They would have to pay for their disobedience, but, like most loving parents, he would love these people whom he had called to be his own. We, too, ignore him. We, too, offend him. Yet he will forgive us, too—if we ask.

Let us pray.

Let your continual mercy, O Lord, rest upon us, for we, too, have ignored you and offended you. Grant, O Father, that we may realize how we misuse our freedom and live contrary to your teachings and example. We ask this in the name of Jesus. Amen.

READ FROM YOUR BIBLE: MICAH 4:2-5

Learning His Ways

In recent years, the school systems in this country have been closely examined. There is general agreement that, from an educational viewpoint, we are falling short of our goals.

Who is responsible? There is plenty of blame to go around. School boards blame the government because they don't receive enough money to do the job. Parents blame the school administrators. Educators blame the parents for not insisting that students spend more time on homework and less time watching television, working, and socializing.

When schools in this country are compared with schools in Japan and Germany, our nation's leaders tell us that our students are falling behind in such basic skills as math, reading, and writing. If the next generation is "high-tech," as many people say it will be, our students, and therefore our country, will be in deep trouble. We may lose our place as the most powerful nation in the world because we cannot keep up with the specialized instruments and machinery of the future.

Today's young people are learning a great deal more than any previous generation—but not all of it is in school. They are learning through television and on the streets of our communities. And *what* they are learning is not what we choose.

Our nation seems to be in deep trouble because we lack a national vision to inspire us *and* the will to bring it to pass. We are people whose dominant national goals seem to be looking for thrills and distractions. We do not, as a people, want to buckle down with determination and discipline to achieve something beyond immediate pleasure.

We look to the schools to inspire such visions in our youth, but the schools cannot do the job alone. The adult population, not just parents but all adults, must also support this national vision. The goals that are presented to our youth today do not emphasize spiritual values like freedom and opportunity, but greed, looking out for number one, and owning the latest in clothes, cars, and the like.

Are these the goals that have made this nation great? Hardly. Compassion and self-sacrifice were the key values during the early years of this country. Today these have been smothered by a mentality that puts "me" first.

* * *
** ** **

The prophet Micah had an acute insight into his nation's religious problem. He lived at about the same time as Isaiah, and, like Isaiah, he used strong language to warn the people against their idolatry, injustice, and lack of penitence. He knew that judgment would fall on the people because of their unrighteousness. They had failed to learn God's ways.

The people who heard his message probably regarded him as a religious fanatic and paid no attention to his warnings. They failed to change, and conditions worsened. A few years later, they probably said, "We should have listened to Micah. He was right after all."

Before we condemn the people who heard Micah's message and disregarded it, we should look to our own situation in our own time. What is God's message to us now? Are we paying attention?

Our schools are not likely to improve as long as groups persist in placing the responsibility on someone else. Our churches will not improve until we face up to our lack of energy in doing God's work.

We have excuses ready always when we have the opportunity to serve. Like the people in Micah's time, we are not yet competent in learning God's way.

Let us pray.

Merciful God, who sent your messengers to warn your people of approaching destruction, may we be attentive to your counsel to us. Help us to be faithful servants, to learn that you seek righteousness, justice, and penitence in your people as signs of their redemption. We ask this in the name of Jesus. Amen.

NOVEMBER 29, 1992

READ FROM YOUR BIBLE: JEREMIAH 8:18-22

Sick at Heart

A bright young man had poor grades because he had not worked hard in his first semester of college in a distant city. He flew into a rage when his father made him withdraw and return home. The father told his son that he would have to study at a local university, where the costs were much lower, and he could live at home until he proved that he was serious enough about his education to work harder and to earn good grades.

The son was so angry that he hit the road. For several years, he worked at various jobs in construction and in the oil fields. He never wrote or called his dad and his anger never decreased.

One evening, when he was almost thirty years old, sitting in a room in a boarding house, he looked back on the ten years he had spent on the road. He thought about the rage he had felt toward his father. Recently, he had begun to think that maybe his dad had been right, that he should have continued his education.

In the next few days, this idea grew in his mind. He decided that he would go back to his father and apologize. Maybe his dad would still help him get an education.

He went back to the city where he had grown up, and, as he drove down the familiar street where he had lived as a boy, he wondered what should be his first words to his father. After he knocked, a stranger came to the door. He asked to see his father. The man told him that he had bought the house five years earlier after the father had died.

In a state of shock, the son drove to the cemetery where his mother had been buried. As he stood looking at his parents' graves, he was sick at heart for the lost opportunity to rebuild a relationship with his father. He had waited too long.

* * *
** ** **

The prophet-priest Jeremiah gave later generations a great deal of information about his feelings as he attempted to fulfill his call. He had been told not to marry and have children, so he was denied the comfort of a family as he faced hostile rulers, priests, and people. Not only did he feel surrounded by personal and political enemies, but he also felt that at times even God had deserted him. He felt an anguish of spirit unmatched by any other prophet. His mission was more than a sacred vocation. He felt deeply for the people who were running toward judgment in the political power plays of the region. He knew that destruction lay ahead, but he could get no hearing with the leadership of either temple or kingdom.

The passage we have heard today expresses the grief of Jeremiah toward the unfaithful and perverse people. He knew what lay ahead for them, but they paid no attention to him. Their realization of his teachings would come too late.

Contrast the attitude of Jeremiah with his sense of disaster that was to come with the attitude of Jonah. Jonah wanted to see the destruction of Nineveh, but he was chastened by God for his hardness of heart. Jeremiah, on the other hand, was immensely dejected and sick at heart because of his compassion toward the people.

We, too, have moments when we are sick at heart because of our impenitence, which blocks our reconciliation with God.

The son who would not return to his father until it was too late experienced the despair of seeking reconciliation too late.

Let us not follow his example.

Let us pray.

Almighty and merciful God, we too, like Jeremiah, have suffered sickness of heart when we have not admitted our uncaring behavior. May we seek you while you may be found, asking pardon for our offenses, in the name of Jesus. Amen.

Strength of the Inner Self

In a subdivision west of Miami, seventy condominiums were built in the late 1980s. Each dream home had all the features that would attract young buyers.

After the homes were sold and occupied, the dreams of these young families turned into a nightmare. One problem was that the buildings had many cracks and leaks. But the worst was yet to come. When the inspectors for the city came to check the repairs, they found a much greater problem: the homes were not built to withstand hurricane force winds as required by Miami codes.

More than two years earlier, county officials said that the homeowners must bring these buildings up to the required level, or they would be torn down.

The owners tried to sue the builders, but they ran into legal problems. Now the case is still in court, but the threat of demolition hangs over the heads of young families. They invested their life savings into these houses, and they lack the necessary money to bring them up to the required standard.

Because the homes do not come up to county requirements, the owners cannot get hurricane insurance. If a storm should come, these houses would almost certainly be destroyed because their walls and other parts of the inner structure were not built to withstand high winds. If the inner framework collapses, the houses will be demolished.

The passage we have heard today is a part of one of the most important books of the New Testament. The Letter to the Ephesians presents God's plan to create a new community of both Jews and Gentiles. In this community, the social and religious barriers that had formerly existed would be abolished. The bond of this unity would be the church.

Paul prays here that the Ephesians will receive power to be strong in their inner selves, that Christ will be at home in their hearts by faith, and that the roots and foundation of this community will be love.

This statement moves from the inner self to the outer community. It suggests an order of events that can guide us. Strength of the inner self comes first.

Where does this strength come from? It comes to us as a gift if we rightly understand the spirituality of the Christian message. Christianity is first a message of the spirit, and all other components follow.

How is this strength gotten? First, it comes from an understanding of how Christ works in the inner life. We gain this understanding primarily by a study of the Gospel accounts of Jesus' life and ministry. In imitation of him, we can develop an approach to life founded on one who went about doing good.

This development of inner strength is essential to all that is to follow when we become disciples of Jesus. If we do not follow his manner of life, and thereby develop this inner power, no amount of doctrinal or biblical knowledge will enable us to become true disciples.

The homes in Miami are beautiful to see. They are built around a small lake. The lake, the clouds, the blue sky, and the pastel colors all present a magnificent picture. Yet in those homes, attractive to behold, lie hidden defects that will lead to their destruction in a hurricane.

Many Christians are blown away when facing a major challenge. They lack the strength of the inner self to shelter them from the storms of life.

Let us pray.

O God, the strength of those who put their trust in you, we long for the inner capacity to prevail against the hurricanes of life. May we be of a single mind to expand this inner strength through a commitment to learn the life of Jesus and to follow his example. We ask this in his name. Amen.

DECEMBER 13, 1992
READ FROM YOUR BIBLE: LUKE 1:67-79

To Guide Our Steps

Every day of every year, thousands of airplanes arrive and depart from American airports. Especially around major cities, called "hubs," the number of moving planes is impressive.

The professionals who keep this traffic in order are air traffic controllers. Operating in towers and at other sites, they use radar screens to keep track of nearly every plane in the air. In the early morning and late afternoon hours, when the travel is most intense, they have their hands full at major airports.

They must monitor not only the airplanes that are in the sky but also those on the ground, approaching or leaving the terminal. Each day, millions of lives depend on the faithfulness of these teams to their tasks.

Occasionally an air traffic controller will make a mistake that will result in an accident, but considering the number of decisions that they make in a year's time, the percentage of error is exceedingly small.

One responsibility they have is to warn pilots of approaching bad weather, either in the sky or at airports. If they spot ominous conditions, they suggest to these fliers a detour that will take them away from the storm and into safer air space. Their equipment is so finely tuned that they can give a pilot instructions on the direction to fly and exactly how long to fly to avoid the threatening storm.

This profession has an extremely high level of stress. Some of these staff members burn out because the weight of their decisions is so great. Most, however, stay at their positions year after year, guiding millions of aircraft to their destinations.

We take for granted these individuals who help provide safe conditions for all persons who fly. Yet they are on duty night and day every day of the year to protect air crews and passengers and to be certain that they arrive safely at their destination.

As we think of Christmas only a few days away, we have a Christian obligation to give serious thought to the deeper meaning of this season. For many people, especially those who have young children in their families, it is a time of joy. For others, however—the lonely, the ill, the depressed—the season is approached with dread, for they may feel that they have little reason to be joyful.

For both groups, however, the deeper message of these days is the same. That is, if we are truly devoted Christians, we will not be caught up in the misleading indications of the season, such as shopping for gifts. One sign of our devotion will be whether we pause in our activities to reflect on the coming of Christ into the world and into our lives.

Perhaps those of us who seem to have little reason to be joyful should spiritually review the way Christ helps us even in our resentment toward those who seem happier or in better circumstances than ourselves.

For every Christian, in whatever situation we find ourselves, the genuine meaning of this season is to be discovered and rediscovered as we reflect on the one who came into the world to guide our steps.

Air traffic controllers guide to safety those who fly. Jesus Christ guides all who pledge allegiance to him to safety both in this world and in the next.

Let us pray.

We thank you, heavenly Father, for your devotion to us through all our days. During this Christmas season, help us to keep our focus on the proper reason for our celebration. May we all, in whatever circumstances we find ourselves, find a reason to be joyful because of the gift of one who guides our steps along the way. We ask this in the name of Jesus. Amen.

READ FROM YOUR BIBLE: LUKE 2:8-20

Amazing Grace

A survey a few years ago found that "Amazing Grace" is the most popular hymn in this country. Even people who do not profess any interest in the Christian faith like its melody. But even religious people who know the words by heart may no longer hear its real message.

Paul Tournier (pronounced TURN-YAY) is a well-known Swiss physician and writer of Christian books. In his book *Creative Suffering,* he says that the starting point of this book on suffering arose from an article by a fellow physician on the topic "Orphans Lead the World."

His friend had studied the lives of famous men and women who had influenced civilization the most. He had made an amazing discovery: Many of these outstanding persons were cut off from one or both parents either literally or emotionally. Among the names on the list were Alexander the Great, Julius Caesar, George Washington, Napoleon, Queen Victoria, and Golda Meir, to name only a few. Some of the most famous people in history had been deprived of the support of one or both parents.

The friend developed a theory based on this study that this emotional loss leads some young people to get into politics. Why? Because the loss of one or both parents and the sense of helplessness that followed led them to seek positions of power when they became adults.

In the book *Creative Suffering,* Dr. Tournier discusses what happens when this will to have power is put to the service of humanity instead of personal greed. For instance, he speaks of Moses, who was in a sense an orphan, since his mother could not claim him. He became the advocate of the Hebrews and led them out of slavery in Egypt.

Dr. Tournier in this book discusses the power he and other physicians have over their patients. This power can be used for healing, or it can be destructive. He describes a scene in which a man tells his doctor that the medicine he is taking has unpleasant side effects. Instead of the physician's trying to understand the feelings of the patient and perhaps changing the medicine, he loses his temper and rebukes the man.

* * *
** ** **

In general terms, grace is one person rescuing another from weakness and a sense of helplessness to overcome it himself or herself. It is the opposite of a reward for good conduct.

The persons referred to earlier who were deprived of the emotional support of one or both parents usually found another person who provided this "grace" for them.

We see grace operating in the attitude of a father or mother toward a small child. The child is too weak and helpless to take care of its own needs, and it lacks means to repay the adult for the care it receives. So the feeling of an older person toward a child illustrates well this idea of grace.

What attitude does the child have toward this care giver when he or she grows up? If the child, now adult, is thoughtful at all, the attitude will be one of amazement that so much was done for a child.

In the passage we have heard today, the people were amazed at the witness of the shepherds. The text conveys that they were amazed that this child would become the messiah.

With the apostle Paul, the amazement is because God accepts persons as righteous and free from guilt if they repent.

We live in a world where few events amaze us. We have seen it all: men walking on the moon, miracle drugs to extend our lives, a level of prosperity that baffles the rest of the world. But on this Sunday before Christmas, we should remain for a few moments in the presence of the Savior, the babe of Bethlehem, whose love we know as grace—amazing grace.

Let us pray.

Almighty God, give us grace on this day to consider the real gift of

Christmas, your Son. May we in these moments of quietness attain a true sense of this season. We ask this in Jesus' name. Amen.

DECEMBER 27, 1992

READ FROM YOUR BIBLE: JOHN 1:19-34

Preparing the Way

Many children want to learn how things are made. To gratify this interest, a book published about two years ago describes how the subways were built in Paris, France.

A civil engineer assigned to the subway project was a humble man. His first big task was to dig the network of underground tunnels for the trains. The workers hit many unexpected problems. They found underground springs, rock quarries, layers of chalk and sand, underground caverns, and prehistoric swamps under the existing city of millions of residents.

The Seine River flows through the middle of Paris, so the subway lines had to go under the river. One big problem was the need to remove the mud of the river bed. The solution was clever. The workers froze the mud solid, then cut it away with picks and axes and hauled it away before it thawed.

The project lasted almost forty years, but the modest engineer in charge of the work stayed with it until it was completed. The French government recognized his talent and leadership by awarding him the Legion of Honor award not once but four times.

Millions of people ride the Paris subway each day, but few know of the humble engineer and the dedicated workers who worked for so long to bring its construction to pass.

* * *
** ** **

Preparing the way is not an easy task. Those who blaze the trails are often subject to ridicule and threats. The scientists who developed inoculation for smallpox and anesthetics were scorned by others.

Today we have read of John the Baptist, forerunner of Christ. The Gospels suggest that John and Jesus were relatives. Perhaps they knew each other as boys and may have played together.

When they grew to manhood, however, John saw his role. He was not an equal to the Christ, but he was a herald. He prepared the way by preaching the gospel of repentance, by condemning the corrupt society of the time, and by announcing the news of the one who was to come.

For his prophetic work, John would later suffer arrest, imprisonment, and finally execution by Herod. Though he must have anticipated such an end, he did not shrink from his calling.

We, too, have the opportunity to prepare the way of the living Christ to enter the hearts and minds of people who are active today. We are to be introducers of other people to the spirit of the Christian life. This representation need not be public or dangerous in the way that John's was. It can be restrained and simple. It can be as natural as helping at a church dinner or as teaching a class of children or as welcoming a visitor or new member to the church.

On this last Sunday of the year, we might all resolve to help prepare the way for someone else.

Let us pray.

Remember, O Lord, those who have prepared the way for us, someone who long ago gave us some word of encouragement that led to our being here today. May we also be instruments by which the way can be prepared for others. We ask this in the name of Jesus. Amen.

The Lord Is Near

The fifteenth century has been called by historians "The Age of Discovery." During this period, the New World was discovered.

Even before the voyage of Columbus, which led to the discovery of the Western Hemisphere, ships of Portugal were scouting the South Atlantic for routes that would lead to India and China. The purpose of these voyages was to look for sources of spices from these countries that brought such high prices in Europe.

One of the captains who was intent on making such discoveries was Bartholomew Dias. Late in the year 1487, Dias set out from Lisbon with three ships to explore the coast of Africa. He ran into a storm that blew his vessels far out to sea. After thirteen days, the tempest ended, and Dias set sail back toward the African coast. Several days later he spotted the coastline and landed his ship in territory that is today a part of the Republic of South Africa.

Dias wanted to go around the southern coast of the continent. If he had done so, he would have discovered the way to India. He would have become one of the most famous men of history, but he did not go far enough. His crew, having almost lost their lives in the storm, would not go farther. Dias had no choice but to return to Portugal. He died a few years later, disappointed that he never had the opportunity to follow through on his earlier voyage.

Our devotional passage for today is a quotation from the Greek version of part of Psalm 16. In it, the writer expresses a confidence that God is always near.

As surprising as it seems at first glance, one of the problems the nations of the ancient world had was knowing whether their gods were paying attention to them. In experiences such as Elijah had on Mount Carmel (see I Kings 18:20 and following for the story) several centuries before the time of Christ, the prophets of Baal could not get the attention of their god to perform a miracle for them.

The prophet Isaiah directs the people to "turn to the LORD and pray to him, now that he is near" (Isaiah 55:6 GNB). This declaration suggests that the people may have sometimes felt that God was far away.

The second chapter of the book of Acts teaches that God is ever present through his Holy Spirit. John Wesley said on his deathbed, "And best of all, God is with us."

This sense of the constant presence of God in the life of the Christian bestows on us immense comfort. There are times in life when no human being can understand what we are passing through, but God can and does.

The tragedy is found when people become frustrated because they do not sense the presence of God. We must always remember that God is not like a porter in a hotel who can be summoned by phone and who comes rushing to fulfill our requests. Seeking the presence of God is itself a capability that must be learned through trial and error.

Often we give up too soon. We, like Bartholomew Dias, may be on the verge of a great discovery, only to give up and turn back.

Teachers of Eastern religions say that the discipline of meditation requires years of practice. Christians must come to the same realization. Learning how to come into the presence of God will not happen overnight.

On this first Sunday of the new year, we celebrate the coming of the Holy Spirit into the early church. We do not stop there; we hope that the Spirit will come into our church and our lives also.

Let us pray.

Almighty and everlasting God, at the start of this new year, we pray that it shall be marked by an increasing closeness with you. May we have the determination to learn the language of the Spirit, so that we

49

may call upon you, since you are near. We ask this in the spirit of Jesus. Amen.

JANUARY 10, 1993

READ FROM YOUR BIBLE: I PETER 2:1-10

Preparing for a Certain Destiny

A hundred years ago, most American denominations experienced impressive growth. New members came to the churches in large numbers, and well-known evangelists drew huge crowds to their services.

Today many churches have trouble holding their own in terms of membership. New church buildings are a rarity, because often it takes several years to raise the funds for the modern structure.

In former ages, churches and cathedrals were often begun with limited funds. When the money ran out, construction stopped. As more funds were raised, the building began anew. Two hundred years was required for the completion of some large churches.

We may ask, "What took so long?" One answer is that the people were poor and had little money to offer. They gave their labor—all that many people had to give. Will Durant, in *Age of Faith,* describes how sometimes thousands of men and women worked side by side to pull the heavy wagons loaded with stones, beams, and other supplies. As they hauled those enormous loads, no voices, no complaints, no expressions of weariness were heard. When they stopped for rest, no conversation was heard, only prayers and confessions of guilt. In such an immense task, "hatred [was] soothed, discord [was] driven away, debts [were] forgiven, unity [was] restored" (G. C. Coulton, *Life in the Middle Ages,* vol. II [Cambridge: Cambridge

50

University Press, 1930), p. 18. The cathedral referred to is in Chartres, a small town fifty-five miles southwest of Paris).

One stone after another, these magnificent buildings were erected, and today, centuries after their completion, they are witnesses to the age of faith.

* * *
** ** **

The text we have heard today states that the living stone—that is, Jesus—was rejected as worthless by the people in his time. Yet God made him the most valuable. The writer also asserts that Christians should be living stones, to be used in the building of a spiritual temple.

This figure of speech suggests that we are to join one another in the erection of this spiritual temple. Individual stones are simply products of a quarry; they are not a building. They must be put together in a fitting way before they become useful for refuge and shelter.

If we prize ourselves individually too highly, we are simply like the stones in the quarry. If we work together, like the poor people in the construction of the great cathedrals, however, we will discover that hatred is soothed, discord is driven away, debts are forgiven, and unity is restored.

In the church, we are preparing for a certain destiny. For that destiny to be realized, we must all become together as building stones in a spiritual temple dedicated to God.

Let us pray.

Almighty God, increase in us the works of faith, hope, and charity, that we may become a spiritual temple and discover the kindness of the Lord. May we also "grow up" in the certainty of faith, acting always as responsible disciples, seeking unity, harmony, and love. We ask this in the name of Jesus. Amen.

READ FROM YOUR BIBLE: EPHESIANS 2:14-22

One in Christ

Can you visualize what it was like to be a Jew in Germany in the early 1930s?

Think about it this way: How would it feel if the government let it be known that every person in your class or race or gender was to be put outside the law? Under these circumstances, any other citizen could harm you in any way he or she wanted, but you could not expect to be protected by the police.

Or suppose the order came out that every person in a certain age group, man or woman, or every person whose ancestors came from a particular country could be publicly mistreated and have his or her property taken or destroyed without recourse to the law? How would it feel to be part of such a group?

The Jews living in Germany must have been terrified on the "night of glass" when their businesses and many of their homes were destroyed as the police merely watched. It was an ordeal that none of us would want to live through.

Imagine the Christians living during the first centuries of the new era under pagan emperors, like Nero, who had followers of Jesus killed by the thousands. Imagine having to meet as a church in the darkness behind locked doors for fear of being discovered. Imagine what it was like to hear a knock at the door and to fear that the dreaded officers were there to take you and your family away to certain death.

Such experiences as these are almost too horrible to imagine, for most of us are accustomed to a freedom that in other ages was only a dream. We do not dread the knock on the door while we are worshiping or studying together. We are protected by our rights as Americans.

You would think that such fright would have kept the churches from growing, but just the opposite is true. In spite of the terror people must have felt, they found a unity in Christ that has been almost unknown in other ages, and the church grew rapidly in times of persecution.

* * *
** ** **

Our text for today provides the foundation for the unity of the church. Christ intended to make Jews and Gentiles one people. Through his death, he broke down the wall that separated people into races or genders or ages and formerly made them enemies. As a result, we are one new people in union with Christ. He came to preach and to live the good news of peace to all. Through him, we are able to come in one spirit into the presence of the Father.

The establishment of unity requires some central person or purpose around which it is fixed. Thus we see political parties, trade unions, business associations, and community groups who have common missions and goals. People who believe in those missions and goals affiliate with such organizations, and in the bonding of their efforts strength is derived.

The church is such an organization, speaking in human terms. We gather because we are convinced of the mission and goal set by Christ long ago. Through almost two thousand years, such ideals have been maintained.

It is this common purpose that unites us. In a negative and destructive way, those who persecuted the Jews were united about the goals of Hitler to establish a master race. We have seen the devastation caused when an evil idea or person becomes an idol.

In the opposite way, we gather around the life and work of Jesus because we want to spread love, not hate, and to be builders, not destroyers.

Let us pray.

Lord God Almighty, in whose name we find our unity through Jesus Christ, help us to remember that your Son broke down all barriers of race and gender and religion so that all who come to him might be a part of his spiritual body, the church. May we as persons realize that all people are our brothers and sisters in your family. We ask this in the name of Jesus. Amen.

JANUARY 24, 1993

READ FROM YOUR BIBLE: I CORINTHIANS 2:1-9

The Secret Wisdom

Michael Landon was one of the most prominent stars of television over the past thirty years. Before he died in 1991, he showed more of his character than many stars want to reveal.

After his terminal illness was diagnosed, he talked with Johnny Carson on "The Tonight Show" about his intention to fight with all the strength he had. He also spoke about bizarre medical treatments he had tried because he was desperate to prolong his life.

When medical authorities told Landon that he had only a short time to live, he responded as many of us would. He wanted to try every possible remedy. Until we have ourselves been in such a bleak position, we cannot know how we would react. It is easy to assume that we would be braver than others who have faced such an ordeal.

We were not told in the press about spiritual resources this star called on. His father was Jewish, so perhaps Landon was able to explore the resources of his ancestors when faced with this crisis. Perhaps he had friends of other faiths who tried to help him.

One thing we know is that to face the frightful prospect of an early death without religious faith is to confront the demon of fear at close range.

* * *
** ** **

The text we have heard today illustrates the attractive modesty of the apostle Paul. (We can admit that his statement

54

in his writings that he is not boasting is a boast itself.) He begins by saying that, when he came to the church at Corinth, he did not come with big words and impressive learning. He said: "I made up my mind to forget everything except Jesus Christ and especially his death on the cross" (I Corinthians 2:2 GNB). He admitted that he was trembling with weakness, so his words did not suggest that he was a skillful orator. What made his message persuasive, he said, was not his eloquence but the power of God's Spirit.

In this age of television entertainment, we have come to think that our teachers and preachers must be at least as well-spoken as Billy Graham. Yet history teaches us that the Spirit does not depend on dazzling speech. When Jonathan Edwards preached his famous sermon centuries ago that began a great revival movement here in this country, people said that he read his sermons in a low voice and hardly ever looked up to face the congregation. Yet when he preached, men and women were deeply affected.

Eloquence is not required; sincerity is. Eloquence brings praise to the speaker, but such praise was not the goal of Paul. He sought conviction, and his modesty and dependence on God enabled him to touch people who otherwise would have been unreachable.

The effectiveness of our testimony will be like that of Paul if we follow his example. We will find that our actions and words will make up in sincerity what they lack in style.

This dependence on God is what Paul called the secret wisdom revealed by God through his chosen messengers and ambassadors. We, too, should rely solely on the power of the Spirit to give content to our testimony.

In addition, our testimony will usually be in the form of our actions, not our words. The wisdom may be carried in our individual actions without a word being spoken.

Let us pray.

Almighty God, fount of all wisdom, we sometimes try so hard to impress others with our eloquence, but we know in our hearts that to use your Word in the effort to gain praise is unworthy of the life of Jesus.

We pray, therefore, that we may be modest in our search, determined to be an example by our actions and unconcerned with the praise of others. We ask this in his name. Amen.

JANUARY 31, 1993
READ FROM YOUR BIBLE: I CORINTHIANS 12:12-27

Alive As One

Baby John, as the nurses in the hospital called him, was not yet a year old when he changed from a crawling, laughing child into a baby whose health was in obvious decline.

The medical team treating him discovered that he had liver failure. In the hospital, the physicians said that unless he received a transplant, he likely would not live another three days. Baby John's name was placed immediately on the transplant register, but the prospect of finding a matching donor seemed impossible in so short a time.

The family was about to give up hope when a telephone call came, saying that a young child had drowned and her parents had offered her organs for the treatment of other children.

Baby John was rushed by chartered plane to Pittsburgh, where the operation was performed the following day. A year later, Baby John, almost two years old, has become an energetic, outgoing child like others his own age.

His family told this story to the newspapers in the hope that other parents could understand the need for organ donations for children. The parents of the little girl who drowned and who provided the liver for Baby John gave life not only to him but to three other children as well. In that way, the child they had loved and lost could live on in other children, who would die unless they received help.

Baby John's grandmother wrote: "If you are one of the very few that has the opportunity to pass life on to another, think of it as the most meaningful gift you've ever given, and a new life for another. What could be a more beautiful final tribute to you or your loved one than to pass on the gift of life?" (*The Westview,* July 12, 1991, p. 8).

* * *
** ** **

Our text for today asserts that one part of the human body by itself is of no use. All the parts must work together to have a living, functioning human being. When one part fails, the entire body begins to break down. To see this breakdown in another human being of any age is heart rending. If we or someone we love is having this experience, we beg for help from anyone who may be in a position to give it. Each year, thousands of people die because transplants are not available. Many young persons especially can pass on the gift of life to others. Tragedy is doubled or tripled because other lives that might be saved are lost.

The loss of a part of the body of Christ, the church, is also tragic. The loss of one part, one individual, may in turn lead to other losses.

A man took his umbrella to church one rainy Sunday. When he got ready to leave after church, his umbrella was not where he had left it. A few Sundays later, he saw someone with an umbrella that looked exactly like his. He became convinced that this person purposely had taken his possession. He became enraged, but he said nothing. He stopped going to church. Others asked him why. He would not tell the whole story, but he said someone had wronged him. His friends believed him, and some of them stopped attending that church. A chain reaction began, and in a year's time more than a dozen people had quit coming to this church. Others had taken sides and created hard feelings. Some stopped going to church completely.

One moral of this story is that one member—one part of the body—can lead to the destruction of other parts of the body. To accomplish the work of Christ in the world, all members must unite and work together.

Let us pray.

Almighty God, giver of all good gifts, as we unite here today in your name, we feel that we are all part of one body. Yet we realize that other parts of your body are missing from our fellowship. Help us to become more committed to bringing others into this group so that they, too, will discover the satisfaction of life as a part of your church. We ask this in Jesus' name. Amen.

Complete the Mission

One of the most thrilling sights in America takes place each year when the service academies—like West Point—have their graduation exercises. In military precision, the young men and women receive their diplomas and their commissions as officers.

Like many other college graduates, some of these young officers have a new experience on this day. Before, their major objective had been to complete their courses of study with grades good enough to allow them to graduate. On the day they get their degrees, however, they realize afresh the commitment they have made in order to receive their education: a commission as an officer in the military forces and a duty to serve their country.

Some of them do not intend to make a career of military service. They applied for admission because they wanted the first-class schooling they would receive. Of course, they intended to follow through on their commitment to serve in the military for the required term, but, after that, they had other plans.

One of our national goals is to provide the best military leadership by offering quality training in the service academies. This goal directs the kind of education these young people receive. It is paid for by the citizens and is free to those who are accepted. Its purpose is not to provide a good general education but to furnish our Army, Navy, Air Force, Marines, and Coast Guard with the best officers.

The basic idea of a "commission" is an agreement between two parties. One will provide goods or services in exchange for some equivalent compensation. In the case we have been describing here, the government offers the education, and the students agree to a term of military leadership.

* * *
** ** **

When the apostle Paul set out on his life's work, he took seriously the requirement to spend his existence on behalf of Christ. He believed that he had received a precious gift; his part of the commission was to go about the world to carry his message to all who would listen.

The book of Acts and his letters describe the events in his life through which he passed in fulfillment of his commission. We marvel at the misfortunes that came about as he devoted his life to this realization.

We are not called to imitate the life of Paul and to suffer the hardships that he experienced. But we are called, commissioned, for a specific purpose. When we join the church, we take a vow to support the church, the body of Christ, with our time, our talents, and our means. If we take this promise seriously, we have a mission in life.

No person can judge whether another person is fulfilling this commission, but we know in our own hearts whether we have taken it seriously.

As citizens, we offer the pledge of allegiance to our nation. As Christians, we pledge allegiance to Christ. Do we take the commission of Christ as seriously as we take our duty as citizens?

Let us pray.

O God, you have brought us to this present moment. We consider now our pledge of allegiance to you. We ask ourselves whether we have been faithful to our commission. We ask this in the name of Jesus. Amen.

FEBRUARY 14, 1993
READ FROM YOUR BIBLE: I CORINTHIANS 9:24-28

The Winner's Crown

Since television has become so widespread, the Olympic games are seen by millions of people. Even people who are not ordinarily interested in sports sometimes take time to watch the best amateur athletes in the world compete for the gold, silver, and bronze medals.

The opening ceremonies of the Olympics are stirring as young people from each country march into the stadium bearing their nations' flags. Those who observe the events, especially on television, see the rapture of the winners and the grief of the losers.

For the winners, the years of practice and commitment pay off. As they stand to receive their medals, they know that their sacrifices have paid off. For the losers, devotion to their sport seems to have been wasted. We can feel both the joy of the winners and the depression of the losers.

For many years, the athletes of the Republic of South Africa were denied the opportunity to compete because their government's racial policies would not allow black African athletes to enter their national competitions. Having removed the racial barriers to taking part, the government of South Africa allows young people of all races to participate. The whole country is gratified that they are again admitted to compete in the most popular athletic events in the world.

* * *
** ** **

In the passage we have read today, Paul speaks about the Christian life, using the image of a race. In this and other countries, races are extremely popular—automobiles, motor-cycles, runners, skiers, swimmers, to name only a few. In these races, there is only one winner (although occasionally there may be a tie). Paul points out that all this competition has as its goal the winning of a crown or medal. He notes that these awards will perish in time.

Christians, however, seek a prize that will not perish but will last forever. Only a prize of this type is worthy of the effort.

Along with the Olympic games every four years, other games, called the Special Olympics, are held more often. These games are for people who have some kind of handicap. Because of the great effort put forth by these contestants, every player receives a reward.

The Christian life is like these Special Olympics. Everyone who enters the race wins an award, the gift of eternal life.

Each winner of the race for the Christian prize—in other words, everyone—has the obligation of seeking other contestants. As we invite others to participate in this new life, we proclaim the gospel. In so doing, we motivate others to seek the crown that does not perish.

Let us pray.

Lord of all might and power, we thank you for the opportunity to participate in the Christian life, in which every person wins a crown. Aid us, we pray, as we make our witness and proclaim the gospel. We ask this in the name of Jesus. Amen.

FEBRUARY 21, 1993
READ FROM YOUR BIBLE: COLOSSIANS 3:1-15

The Old Life and the New

Persons who today are middle-aged have seen a revolution in human life since they were born. Who could have guessed thirty or forty years ago that today we would learn routinely of major organ transplants, that an airplane could cross the Atlantic Ocean in under four hours, that the planet Mars could be photographed and those photos sent back to the United States, or that you could receive thirty channels on your television set?

Who would have thought that computers would be used in so many ways, that you could use a plastic credit card to pay for merchandise you ordered on the telephone from distant cities, that you could record a program appearing on television and play it back any time you wanted to, that gasoline would ever cost more than thirty cents a gallon, that a loaf of bread would ever cost more than a quarter, that something called a microwave oven could bake a potato in six minutes, that a new car would cost in 1993 more than the average house cost in 1960, that earth satellites thousands of miles in the sky could photograph and make visible an object on earth no larger than a bread box? Who would have guessed that today neither men nor women wear hats as they formerly did?

Surprises like these cause us to reflect on the changes the world will see before another thirty years have passed. If your great-grandparents could see the world today, they wouldn't believe their eyes. And if we could return to the earth a hundred years from now, we would probably not believe our eyes either.

One of the problems that faces all of us today is what was has been called "future shock." Changes are so rapid that we cannot absorb them. People living today will see more changes in their lifetime than generations would have seen a few years ago.

One of the greatest changes we have seen in modern times is the system of values by which society lives. Violence is everywhere. Human life has been cheapened. Men and women in government and other places of responsibility are exposed for having put personal gain ahead of service and deceived the public and their employers. Scandals are so abundant that magazines have made millions by revealing facts that might not have reached the public otherwise. Television evangelists have devastated viewers who sent them money by living in a luxurious style and engaging in questionable moral practices.

At the same time, progress has been remarkable. Persons who would have died a generation ago are able to live longer and more fruitful lives because of new medicines and techniques. Satellite weather systems warn people of storms that could be dangerous in sufficient time for them to seek shelter. Television has enabled us to see and hear government and other public figures around the world at the very instant they are speaking. We see programs of news, public information, and entertainment on television that are free to the viewer.

* * *
** ** **

Our text for today helps us to see that in a world that is changing rapidly some things do not change. The values Paul speaks about in this chapter do not go out of style. Once, every man and woman who came to church thought he or she had to wear a hat to be well dressed. Though hats are today coming back into style for women and men, they are still rare enough to cause a comment in some places.

Paul warned the people that the desires they formerly felt were a part of their old lives and had no place among those who were dedicated to Christ. The old life and all its values had to be cast away forever; the new value system had replaced it. In this passage, he sets forth the outlook by which every follower of Jesus should live.

Let us remember that in a changing world, some things do not change. Our commitment to Christian values remains in spite of all other changes. These values will be as valid a century from now as they are today.

Let us pray.

Give us grace, O Lord, to distinguish between the values that are eternal and those in our daily lives that may change from time to time. May we be faithful to our heritage we have received from Jesus, in whose name we pray. Amen.

FEBRUARY 28, 1993

READ FROM YOUR BIBLE: TITUS 2:11-14

Eager to Do Good

The elderly man, past ninety years of age, had moved to a new town to be nearer his children. He got an apartment of his own so he could continue to conserve as much independence as possible. The church he decided to go to was only a short distance from his apartment.

He missed his former church in the smaller community where he had lived all his life. He rode to church with a neighbor. People were nice to him, but moving at his age was a big adjustment to make.

One Wednesday evening, after the Bible study class had concluded, he waited for his neighbor to bring the car up to the church steps. He noticed a child, only six or seven years old, a few feet away, looking at him intently. After a moment, she walked up to him, extended her hand, and said in a clear voice, "Hello. I want to be your friend. I'm glad you are coming to our church."

From that moment on, he felt appreciated in his new surroundings. The little girl, who was the granddaughter of his neighbor, wrote him a letter the next week. At every service, she came to speak to him.

She showed that at a very early age she had already learned the principal message of Jesus, as exemplified in his own life. He went about doing good.

Some people think they cannot be worthy Christians because they do not understand complicated doctrines. They feel that they cannot express their faith in words, and they regard this as a weakness, a failure.

The text we have heard today and the major lesson suggests that a person who is too puffed up with knowledge may be detested. Such persons may convey a sense of conceit and arrogance. Correct ideas are, of course, of major importance to the teaching vocation, but not every Christian is called to be an expert in theology.

The best doctrine is found in the example of life. For that reason, some Christians have been called "walking sermons." Their lives are their testimony, and no one who observes them has any doubt about the quality of their faith.

The tragedy of conceit in the church is that it sometimes leads to disputes, which, in turn, lead to hurt feelings and rejection. Argument itself wins very few converts to the Christian church.

Controversy is to be avoided wherever possible. People have the right to differ on matters of faith. Their views should be heard with the same respect as those of anyone else's. Differences should be discussed with tolerance, courtesy, and affection for one another.

Beyond such discussions of doctrinal points, however, is the far more important matter of the way we live. Someone has said that our real religion is what we do and say when we think no one is watching.

The little girl showed the elderly man that she had already learned the fundamental lesson of being a Christian. She could not have expressed her belief in words, but she knew already how to live her faith. She had been taught in watching others.

Doing good is the first responsibility of every Christian. That is the test of our faith. So let us not worry if we feel we lack the words to say all that we believe. The way we live is what counts.

Let us pray.

Almighty and eternal God, by whose mercy we come to this present hour, help us to be aware of the quality of our lives, that we are teaching others by the way we live. Forgive us when we engage in vain debates. Lead us instead to remember that the way to follow Jesus is to go about doing good, as he showed us by the example of his own life. We ask this in his name. Amen.

READ FROM YOUR BIBLE: JOHN 1:19-28

Who Are You?

About two years ago, a movie was produced whose central character was an aggressive attorney in the prime of his life. His existence was altered radically, however, when he was shot accidentally in the head. As a result, he totally lost his memory.

As the film progressed, it showed the dramatic attempts of a man to rediscover who he was. He had to learn to walk, to talk, to rediscover his family and friends. In the process, he began to live by a different system of values than he had held as an autocratic lawyer.

The people in this man's life had to reexamine their existence and relationships. Some of these characters did not change, and the contrast between their lives and the reality of their former friend and coworker was especially powerful. The first question they asked was "Who are you?" but that was followed by "Who am I?"

Implicit in the film was this question: Must we face a life crisis before we can discover who we are?

More and more people are raising this issue in the middle and later years of life. We expect young adults to deal with this question, but usually, we expect to have an exact answer before we enter middle age. In a rapidly changing world, however, we find that we must continue asking this question: Who are we anyway?

Our text today deals with John the Baptist. He was getting a reputation with the Jewish leaders in Jerusalem, and they sent a committee to ask him, "Who are you?"

For centuries, the Jews had been hoping for and expecting the coming of the messiah. They believed that this person would become the new king of the Jews, would reestablish the kingship of David, and would free their country from Roman domination. They expected that a forerunner would come before the messiah. This herald would be Elijah or another prophet.

When the committee from Jerusalem asked him about his identity, John the Baptist declared that he was the voice of one crying in the wilderness, the messenger who was preparing the way of the Lord.

We take this text for granted, so we fail to ask the question that stands behind what we have read: How did John discover his own identity?

The Scripture is silent on details of how John came to this understanding, but our general knowledge of the Bible assures us that probably it was through study of the word and through deep meditation and reflection on his own calling. Jesus and Paul also seem to have gone through such a period in which they sought the will of God for themselves.

Each of us also must deal with the question of who we are. We can define ourselves in a number of ways: by our parents, by our spouse, by our work, or by other achievements. When a new acquaintance asks you about yourself, what is the first thing you talk about? The answer to this question gives a clue to your basic identity.

John's character was affirmed by the work he undertook as a forerunner. He was not the messiah. But he was preparing the way for the messiah.

Should not this vocation be a basic part of our identity also? Are not we also forerunners for him?

Let us pray.

Almighty and eternal God, who searches the hearts of your children, may we discover in the stillness of our meditation who we are. May we also, like John, be forerunners for Christ wherever we go. We ask this in Jesus' name. Amen.

READ FROM YOUR BIBLE: JOHN 3:22-26

How Can This Be?

One of the strangest ideas in the history of religions is the idea of the transmigration of souls—that is, the belief that the soul can leave a person's body during the night and roam around the earth while the individual is asleep.

Related to this idea is the concept that an individual's soul may be reborn in another person. Shirley MacLaine, the actress, has written books about past lives she has lived as other persons.

This idea of the movement of the soul goes back to Egyptian times, and it is also found in some Eastern religions. The earliest idea was that the soul can leave the body during sleep and return before the person awakens. This belief probably arose because people did not understand the true nature of dreams. They thought that their dreams reflected events that actually happened while they were asleep.

Later, the theory arose that if the soul could leave the individual during sleep and could reenter the person before awakening, then the soul could enter and be reborn in another individual.

In ancient Greece, people believed that the soul survived physical death and was punished or rewarded, according to the type of life the person had lived. Later this soul would be restored to another human living at a later time. After the soul had lived through three lifetimes on earth, it might find ultimate release. Another idea of this same period was that when the soul was purified it returned to the company of the gods.

* * *
** ** **

Although this view was held in some places at the time Jesus lived, it is certainly not what he taught. In our text for today, he spoke to Nicodemus about a new birth, but he was not teaching that the soul migrates into another person.

What is taught here is that the soul must be reborn from God, who imparts a new spirit into the person. The condition of this new birth is a conviction or faith in Christ. The understanding here is that an individual becomes a child of God, then becomes a new creation, then shares in the divine nature, and ultimately shares in Christ's victory over sin and death according to the depth of one's faith.

In our time, we sometimes hear persons bragging about having been "born again" or being "born-again Christians." Such boasting is totally out of character with the nature of the process of regeneration, which is the doctrine of the new birth. One characteristic of this new birth is to refrain from such boasting. Humility is one of the basic characteristics of the new birth, so strutting around and showing off express lack of Christian maturity and in-depth understanding of what is supposed to happen.

Many people, unfortunately, feel locked into some old form of life. The teaching of our passage for today is that this process of new birth or regeneration is open to every Christian who has faith in Christ.

How can this be? It is through the gift of Jesus Christ that it occurs, not because of any merit on our part. Therefore, let us show our new birth by our deeds rather than by our words.

Let us pray.

Almighty God, because we have no power in ourselves to help ourselves, we look to you for relief and nurture. May we experience a new birth as we seek to revive our priorities and values in life, and may we find comfort in the realization that you bring us to new life. We ask this in the name of Jesus. Amen.

READ FROM YOUR BIBLE: JOHN 8:31-38

The Brilliance of the Son

Less than two years ago, some people in the Western Hemisphere were able to see a total eclipse of the sun. Many television stations showed the event as it was actually happening, so it was visible all over the United States, although the only state where a person could have seen this eclipse was in Hawaii.

A solar eclipse occurs when the moon moves between the earth and the sun so that the light from the sun is partially blocked. In a total solar eclipse, the moon seems to cover the sun entirely for about four minutes. As this eclipse begins, the earth gradually darkens as the moon advances across the sun. When the moon fits exactly over the sun, the light on earth from the sun is about the same as moonlight when the moon is full.

Gradually the process reverses itself as the moon moves away from the sun, and full daylight is restored.

This event causes various reactions. Animals and birds sometimes think that night has come. Dogs will bark because of some distant sense of apprehension of this unusual event.

When the eclipse was visible in Hawaii, thousands of Americans went from the mainland to see this spectacle. A full solar eclipse will not occur again in this country until about the year 2015.

In ancient times, before modern science explained the event, a total solar eclipse terrified people who saw it. Unexpectedly, the sky would become dark. They thought that the end of the world had begun. Today scientists have explained and illustrated what occurs, but the wonder still fascinates us.

Jesus referred to himself as the light of the world. Of course, he meant this description in a symbolic sense. Some were shocked by his claims, while others seemed to accept his message immediately.

In the passage we have read today, Jesus laid down a standard of discipleship to Jews who believed in him. He told them that if they continued in his word—that is, if they continued to have faith in him—they would know the truth, and that truth would make them free.

In the lifetime of Jesus, Palestine was under the rule of the Romans. The desire for freedom was strong among the people, and from time to time, as in modern Europe and the Soviet Union in recent years, the desire for freedom got the government's attention.

The contrast Jesus was drawing here is a spiritual one, however, not a political one. He was contrasting slavery to sin with spiritual freedom.

A philosopher began a book once with these words: "Man is born free but is everywhere in chains."

Though this writer was speaking in a general sense, his words can be applied to the spiritual life. Many people today—even church people—think they are free, but they are enslaved to modern values. Two characteristics in society today are hatred and greed. The violence in our society is sometimes caused by the hatred of one person or group for another person or group who is different. Greed is also a harmful outlook on life. Some people become so greedy that they seek far more money or possessions than any one person needs.

If we become true disciples of Jesus, we discover that freedom that only a spiritual commitment can give. We are freed from the slavery of our love for possessions and dislike of others who are different from ourselves.

People who try to look directly at the sun, even during an eclipse, run the risk of destroying their eyesight forever, for sunlight is so intense that the eyes can be burned beyond repair. But when we look at the Son—spelled with an *o*—we find that we win our freedom.

Let us pray.

Almighty and everlasting God, give us an increase of faith, that we may experience the light of Christ. In his light, all things become clear, and our values are elevated according to his will. We put away forever worldly standards by which millions live. We thank you for the freedom granted through your Son, in whose name we pray. Amen.

READ FROM YOUR BIBLE: JOHN 11:45-54

Saved or Ruined?

The South American country of Brazil is huge, and some parts of it have never been fully explored. In one part of the vast nation a state of nature prevailed, and civilization had not touched it. Only a few people knew about it, and therefore visitors were few. No pollution by chemicals or other human products had marred this undefiled paradise.

The situation began to change when a television network went there to film a soap opera. Thousands of viewers found out about this place, and travel agents began to get requests for trips there.

Today the natural beauty is being destroyed by the encroachment of humanity on this place. Hotels are being built there, and pollution of the area has already begun. A once quiet, clean river runs through the region. Sight-seeing boats bring in hundreds of people, who throw trash in the river. Noise and fumes have driven away many of the rare birds who once were found there. In other words, a paradise is slowly being destroyed.

We think of our own United States. A generation or two ago, people could drink from many of the streams and rivers of our country. The air was pure, and no one worried that his or her new home had been built on top of a disposal area for deadly chemicals. Today experts tell us that we must change our ways, because the damage to the environment is getting out of hand.

* * *
** ** **

In our text for today, a plot was begun by the adversaries of Jesus. The reason given for their resistance was that they feared that if the masses of people began to believe in Jesus' mission, the Romans would take his popularity as a sign that a rebellion has been planned. If that should happen, they imagined that both the Temple would be destroyed and the citizens would be killed or scattered. (We must remember that Judea at that time was occupied by a domineering foreign government, much like Kuwait during the Persian Gulf War.)

The irony of this situation is that the one who came to save was accused of being an instrument of destruction. As events would later prove, Jesus was sacrificed in place of a real criminal. The Jews were hoping for the appearance of the messiah who would free them from Roman domination, but the high priest, who was charged by the Romans with keeping the Jews in a peaceful attitude, could not risk letting Jesus become the center of a revolt.

As events occurred, Jesus was crucified and the kingdom of God he hoped to establish was rejected by the Jews. They thought they were saving themselves, but the decision they made led to their destruction.

Today's Christians must also work for the establishment of the kingdom of God—that is, for God's will to be done on earth. Yet, this is hardly a goal for many people who are in church regularly. Primarily many people are there because of an interest in their own salvation. They have little or no interest in anyone or anything else.

A tropical paradise in Brazil is being destroyed by selfishness and greed. The kingdom of God—the key to authentic life—is corroded by these same attitudes.

Jesus offers salvation and life. Those who reject his message and the example of his ministry, whether they are in the church or outside, reject salvation and in doing so are condemned to ruin.

Let us pray.

Almighty and everlasting God, who, by your tender love has made the offer of salvation, our rejection of your way grieves us when we remember the compassion you had for all people. May we avoid the road to ruin and find the way to true discipleship. We ask this in the name of Jesus. Amen.

READ FROM YOUR BIBLE: JOHN 13:31-36

"Do As I Have Done"

Many people today believe that we have few or no heroes or heroines in our time. Even public figures who were respected a few years ago have become suspect after their deceit has been revealed.

In the past, heroes played a prominent part in history. Napoleon was such a man.

About two hundred years ago, near the time when our own nation fought for independence, the French also had a revolution. Theirs began in 1789. For ten years, that country was in turmoil. In November, 1799, Napoleon, only thirty years old but already a general in the army, became head of the nation. A few years afterward, he crowned himself Emperor of France.

Napoleon was a brilliant general who conquered almost all of Europe. The people loved him as a hero. Even after he began to lose some of the countries he had conquered, the people did not desert him. Finally, however, he lost political support and was forced to abdicate in 1814, only fifteen years after he had fulfilled his grand dream. He was forced to go to a small island off the coast of France. Formerly he had been master of Europe. Now he ruled only a few square miles.

Yet, the people had not seen the last of Napoleon. In March of the following year, he landed in southern France. The people forgot all the disaster and defeats of previous years, the wholesale slaughter of thousands of soldiers under his command, and they welcomed him as a returning hero. In less than three weeks, he was again in Paris.

For a hundred days, he renewed in the people dreams of peace and liberty and in his soldiers, the dream of victory. On June 12, 1815, he left for Belgium, and on June 18 he was decisively defeated at the Battle of Waterloo. Yet, he was and is still a hero to the French. He would live the remainder of his life on an island in the Atlantic Ocean off the coast of Africa.

"It would appear that in order to strike the imagination of mankind a hero's life should end with a great misfortune. If he had died a natural death in his palace, or fallen on the field of battle, Napoleon would never have become to posterity the figure we know. Lives like his must end in martyrdom, which crowns them with pity caused by human suffering and the respect due to misfortune" (*Encyclopedia Britannica*, 1957 edition, "Napoleon I," vol. 16, pp. 92-93).

* * *
** ** **

Christians regard Jesus as a hero. He lived a blameless, unselfish life. His only ambition was to bring to people the good news. Though he never harmed anyone, he was himself subject to betrayal and violence. He, who went about doing good, was himself mistreated.

Jesus knew that he was on a collision course with the strongest religious institution in Judea, the high priest. He knew from past experience that the temple authorities would join with the Romans to crush any threat to their control. Yet, Jesus did not hesitate for a moment to face these forces allied against him.

Today most people are reluctant to "get involved," especially with unpopular causes. We put our own well-being first. This attitude is understandable, and in some cases it can be justified.

For others, however, this attitude is a failure of nerve. We have come now to the week in which we will follow the events in the life of Jesus that led to his death. During this week, perhaps, we will think more deeply about his offering of himself to die, and, in doing so, find new strength and courage to do as he did.

Let us pray.

Almighty and everlasting God, grant that we may perfectly follow your will, even as Jesus did. May we follow his example in making our commitment to you a reality in our own lives, that we may do as he did. We ask this in his name. Amen.

The Gift of Peace

Try to imagine, if you can, the situation of Thomas More. He had for many years served his government well. He was a Christian of deep faith whose daily life was directed by his devotion to Christ.

King Henry VIII wanted to commit an act contrary to Christian teaching, so he asked More for advice. Thomas More told him exactly what he thought, that the action was wrong.

The response did not suit the king, so he had Thomas More imprisoned. Because the king was known to be merciless against those who opposed him, Thomas More knew that he would eventually be executed.

He was in prison for two years. During that time, his family begged him to agree with the king so that he could be released, but Thomas More was a man with a sturdy conscience. In spite of the pleas of his family, he remained in prison, knowing well that he at last would pay with his life.

While he was in prison, he wrote a book of consolation. In part, he wrote it for himself, for he faced daily the thought of the end of his own life. He was seeking an inner peace in the prospect of death.

But he also wrote it for his family, to help them understand the reason why he had to obey his conscience. He knew they also needed a sense of peace.

The title of this volume is *A Dialogue of Comfort Against Tribulation,* and it is one man's search for peace when faced with a frightful future.

Using our imagination, let us try to go back to the evening of the first Easter Sunday as described in our text for this day. Earlier that Easter day, some of those who had been closest to

Jesus had discovered the empty tomb. The Christ had appeared to Mary Magdalene. Sunday evening, as the ten disciples were in a locked room—because they were afraid of the Jewish authorities—Christ came and stood among them. Why ten disciples? Because Thomas was not with them, and Judas was no longer a disciple.

Christ's first words were words of comfort. "Peace" was his message for them. Of course, that was the usual Jewish greeting between friends, but on this occasion it had a special meaning. The disciples had been stunned at the sudden trial and death of Jesus. They were still trying to deal with the shock of the events of the past three days. He was gone forever, they thought. Now he stood in their midst.

It is quite impossible for us to imagine the emotion they felt at that moment, for now everything changed. He was back with them again.

Thomas More felt that same presence while he endured two years in prison, facing execution. Christ came into that locked prison and visited him. Christ has visited countless other men and women during these centuries since the first Easter. And he comes to us today in a similar way.

When the dark night of the soul comes to us, he will be present. That was his promise that first Easter, and it is his promise to everyone who has faith in him.

Let us pray.

Ever-living Father, watchful and caring, our source and our end, today your whole church celebrates the victory of Jesus, your Son and our Savior. May we, too, experience the peace that his presence brings in the dark nights of our soul, when we are fearful behind locked doors. May we carry always in our hearts his words of peace. We ask this in his name. Amen.

We Belong to the Truth

A new president was appointed to a church community college in a Midwestern city. When he arrived, he found that the college was on the brink of bankruptcy. He knew that more than first aid was needed if the school was to survive, so he developed, with the assistance of some local business leaders, a long-range plan.

The decision was made that this small college could not compete with the nearby state university. Most young people who had just graduated from high school were already well served by other colleges, so the new president decided that he could not compete in this "market." Some role had to be found that would be unique to this school.

After some months of planning, the decision was made that the new emphasis would be on adult education. For these programs, no one under the age of twenty-three would be admitted.

Other innovations were made. For instance, classes were set up in various buildings around the city so adults would not have to travel to a single campus. Text books were delivered at home to students who ordered them from the central bookstore.

In the decade that has passed, the college has not only become self-supporting, but it also usually has a small financial surplus each year. Buildings on the main campus have been remodeled, a new cafeteria has been built, new lighting has been installed.

The college specializes in helping adults who must also work while they go to school, and its reputation has grown. Now local businesses offer classroom space and financial contributions from time to time. More than eight thousand students now attend the school. At a time when many colleges are facing severe financial problems, this one is prospering because it has found a unique way to serve.

* * *
** ** **

The passage we have heard today expresses confidence and courage in God's presence. These moods arise out of our conviction that if we love God we will do his will. "If a rich person sees his brother in need, yet closes his heart against his brother, how can he claim that he loves God? My children, our love should not be just words and talk; it must be true love, which shows itself in action" (I John 3:17-18 GNB).

To belong to the truth means that we love God and show this love through all we do. It also means that we find the place where we can offer our gifts and talents to help those in greatest need.

A small college on the brink of collapse found new life in finding a special place of service. We also find new life when we discover the situation in which we can best demonstrate the love of God.

When we confirm this love through our actions toward those in need, we testify that we belong to the truth.

Let us pray.

Almighty and everlasting God, whose loving hand has given us all that we have, help us remember that to love is to serve. May we follow the example of our Lord, who did not regard himself as one to be served, but who gave us the pattern of love of others. We ask this in his name. Amen.

READ FROM YOUR BIBLE: JOHN 6:22-29

The Bread from Heaven

At any one time, millions of Americans are on diets. Some of these people have let themselves get totally out of control, and they become desperate to lose a few pounds.

An officer had done good work for twenty-one years on the police force, but he weighed almost one hundred pounds more

81

than he had when he entered the force. A new chief of police decided that all officers who were more than a certain percentage overweight would be required to spend time in the police gym to lose the weight.

The officer made a big effort, but it was not enough. Because he was a good policeman, the chief sent him to a counselor who specialized in weight problems. This counselor helped the man to see that stress in his life was his big problem, not his appetite.

Over a period of months, the counselor helped the man to sort out the problems and to recognize that his overeating was not from hunger. He ate when he was not hungry, and he ate huge amounts. The night his son was arrested for selling drugs, the officer went home and ate a half-gallon of ice cream. For most of his life on the police force, he had reacted to stress by overeating. When he learned to handle his stress better, he was able to lose weight and to get to the level suggested by the police chief.

In recent times, emphasis has been placed on dealing with problems that cause overeating. If people eat when they are not hungry, some other mental or emotional problem may be the cause.

* * *
** ** **

Many Christians are in this same kind of trouble. They think of themselves as good Christians. Don't they go to church and Sunday school regularly? Don't they say a blessing at meals? Don't they pay liberally to the church and other good causes?

Even if the answers to these questions are yes, these persons may still experience a deep longing, an emptiness, that suggests to them that they are not on the right spiritual track.

In such cases, the problem may be in the lack of a total commitment. Persons often enter the church with certain unspoken, and perhaps unknown, reservations. They want to be church people, but they do not want to get too involved

82

personally, and they do not want to make any sacrifice. They want a good life, unhindered by any outside commitment.

Such a person is trying to gain the fruit of the Christian faith without planting the seed. The planting of the seed requires that our commitment be total. We cannot expect to find spiritual peace when we are still looking mostly to our own comforts to bring us the satisfaction we need in life.

If that is the case, the spiritual bread we are eating is not adequate. We must make a deeper pledge to serve God through the church and to hold back nothing of ourselves. If we attempt to make reservations, we cannot find the satisfaction we long for.

How does this work? Suppose we are presented with the opportunity to go to a nursing home one Sunday afternoon a month with others to offer a devotional. Not more than an hour of our time will be required. But suppose also that we like our Sunday afternoons to ourselves, to watch football or some other television program or to work in the garden or workshop.

If we reject this opportunity, or others like it, we are withholding our commitment to take Christ to others. We are letting our selfishness obstruct spiritual food and fulfillment.

Christ offered bread for eternal life. Let's not reject that bread for the bread and values offered by the world, which do not satisfy our deepest hunger.

Let us pray.

Almighty and everlasting God, for our daily bread and every other gift, we give you thanks, but let us not turn away from the bread of eternal life. May we examine our commitment to you and hold back nothing that will leave us empty and unfilled. We ask this in the name of the bread of heaven, Jesus Christ. Amen.

The Witness

In the parking lot of the city auditorium in a large city, a man was beating a woman. He threatened to kill her if she didn't get in the car with him. Hundreds of people passed by and saw the scene, but no one came to the woman's aid, and the police were not called until the man had killed her with a rifle.

Near a busy city street in a public park, a man was abusing a little girl. Hundreds of cars passed, and many people saw what was happening, but they didn't stop, nor did they seek help.

A man had just pulled through an intersection. Looking in his rear-view mirror, he saw two cars collide at that intersection. He stopped his car and started back to see if he could help. Then he changed his mind, got back in his car, and went on his way.

A woman testified in a court case as an eyewitness to a crime. After the defendant had been convicted, a newspaper report was published in which the man said that he would get even with this woman when he got out of prison. His sentence has been nearly served, and he will soon get out. The woman is extremely nervous that this man will make good on his threat.

A man attended a conference of church members of his denomination. One night, after the evening session, he walked into the cabin where he was staying and found several men he knew gambling. He was opposed to gambling, but when they asked him to join in, he did so because he didn't want to be criticized.

In the text we have read today, we find the account of a man who is best known in the New Testament as a witness. John the Baptist did not shirk his obligation to point others to Christ. He was not afraid of criticism. He had no fear of the revenge of others. If he was fearful in any way, he did not let it hinder him. Later he would pay with his life for his testimony to Jesus.

In the accounts conveyed above, the viewpoint that is common to each is the fear of witnessing. People today often do not want to become involved, especially if there is the possibility that the involvement may cause them any uneasiness or discomfort. Too often we have seen a person who wants to be a good Samaritan end up on the losing side.

What is the main hindrance to being a good witness for Christ? Like the illustrations earlier, the individual's concern for his or her own safety and comfort is paramount. This concern is understandable. Yet, we must not allow it to block our testimony to Jesus. We must not walk away from the opportunity to do good. If we do, we are doing the opposite of what Jesus did during his earthly ministry.

Each of us must summon the courage to be a good disciple and to speak up for Christ. In the Gospel of John, Jesus promised to be our advocate with the Father. If he is going to be our friend and guarantor, must we not be his today?

Let us pray.

Almighty and everlasting God, who commissioned disciples to be your witnesses, give us courage to speak the word or to do the deed that will be our own modest and quiet witness to the role of Christ in our lives. Forgive us when we are ashamed to mention the name of the one who went to the cross as our Savior and Redeemer. We pray in his name. Amen.

READ FROM YOUR BIBLE: MATTHEW 19:16-24

Found, Then Lost

The war in Vietnam ended twenty years ago, but one group of Americans has never reached a state of peace. They are the families of men who were reported as missing in action and whose remains have never been found. If their loved ones died in that war, they want to know where they are buried. The remains of some of those who have been missing have been returned from time to time, but many others have never been heard from.

A few years ago, a group of Americans who are veterans of that war decided to go back to that area to see if they could get any information on more than two thousand men who have never been heard from since they disappeared.

Once in a while, some person will return from Southeast Asia and will say that he or she has heard rumors that some of these men are still alive and are being held prisoner. The wife of one of those missing soldiers said that she will never find peace until she knows what happened to her husband. As it is, she doesn't know if she is a widow or not.

Many of these families continue to write government officials and to use every possible means to learn what happened to their fathers, husbands, or sons. They do not feel they can go ahead with their lives until their questions are at last answered.

The passage we have heard today presents one of the most tragic episodes in the Gospels. A young man who seemed to have every material possession in life had not yet found peace in his soul. He wanted to know how to inherit eternal life. Therefore, he asked Jesus a question on this subject.

Jesus responded with a short summary of the Ten Commandments. The young man's answer was that he had kept all of them since his youth. Then he sought further advice, but he was not prepared for the answer Jesus gave. Jesus advised him to sell his goods and give the proceeds to the poor. The young man went away despondent because he could not part with his treasure.

In this brief episode, we see a young man who had won a place in the kingdom of God for a moment because he had followed the commandments all his life. But when he asked Jesus what else might be required, he could not concede the cost. One moment, he seemed to be inside, but in the next, he cast himself out. Once he was found; almost immediately he was lost.

American families with relatives who have been missing since the Vietnam war endure the lostness, for the prize they seek—news of their loved one—has never been received. They are helpless to do more.

The rich young man, like many of us, held the power of obedience in his own hand. He thought he wanted eternal life, but, as it turned out, he wanted his possessions more.

Today many people in our nation and in our community weigh these same questions. They want the security of the spiritual life, but they will not sacrifice other values that have been at the center of their lives. They are pulled both ways, but sometimes, unfortunately, the spiritual outlook loses out to material or other self-centered values.

This scene ends with the young man walking away from Jesus in a state of distress, to be heard from no more. But we must not get sentimental over his plight. Instead, we must study our own.

Let us pray.

Almighty and eternal God, who searches the hearts of your people and who examines our values, we see the tragedy of a young man who seemed to be so near the kingdom, but who turned away because the cost of discipleship was too high. May we explore our own commitments, and renew our allegiance to our Lord and Savior. We ask this in his name. Amen.

READ FROM YOUR BIBLE: JOHN 4:43-54

Welcome!

Almost two years ago, a volcano in the Philippine Islands erupted near Clark Air Force Base. The air base was evacuated, because the volcano might flare again over the next several years.

Opinion in the Philippines is divided over the continued presence of American air and naval bases in that country, but many citizens there want the Americans to stay.

Near Clark Air Force Base is the town of Angeles. It has almost three hundred thousand inhabitants, most of whom depend directly or indirectly on the air base for their livelihood. In some ways, Angeles looks like an American town because McDonalds, Pizza Hut, Dunkin' Donuts, Kentucky Fried Chicken, and many other American businesses are there.

The people of Angeles do not want their city to become a ghost town, so they welcome the presence of the Americans. More than forty thousand Filipinos are employed at the air base. There is even a Baptist church in Angeles, though most people are Catholics. The Baptists have about three hundred members, but about half are Americans. Offerings dropped from $1,500 a week to less than $300 after the base was closed temporarily.

In many countries in the world, American businesses are wanted because they provide jobs for so many local people. Without our military bases, many of these areas will return to poverty. Therefore, the Americans are welcome as long as they want to stay.

Our text for today describes the welcome Jesus had when he returned to Galilee. His early ministry was in that district, and his first miracle was performed at the wedding feast in the village of Cana. The Gospels record (see Mark 6:4) that when Jesus returned to his hometown of Nazareth, he was rejected. There he made the statement that a prophet was not welcome in his own country.

Our passage for today states that on this occasion he was welcomed in this region because the people there had been to Jerusalem and had testified to what he had done there during the Passover.

What do you think would happen if Jesus were to come here to our community? What if he went to places where people are ashamed of what they do? What would happen in the big cities of this country if he went into the bars, taverns, casinos, and crack houses? Would people who are attracted to those places repent of their vices and follow him—or would they turn on him and try to harm him?

We may be sure that during his ministry Jesus went to many places where he was not welcomed. We know of some: He was not welcomed in his hometown; he was not welcomed in the temple in Jerusalem, where he denounced the money-changers; he was not welcomed by the well-to-do in places where he denounced the oppression of the poor.

What kind of welcome do we give him? Would we be glad to have him spend the day with us, to hear our conversations with everyone, to watch us as we relate to other people, to see the books and magazines we read and the television programs we watch? Or would we have some moments of guilt and shame? Would we have to say, "Excuse me, Jesus," or make apologies for the language we use or for our thoughts?

Most of us would probably have such moments. This is not to say that any of us are really bad people; it is merely that we are not yet to the place where we would welcome Jesus every minute of every day.

When Jesus is welcomed, mighty works take place. In the Gospels, when he was not welcomed, we are told, he could do no mighty works in that vicinity.

How about in *this* vicinity? Do we welcome him so he can do mighty works among us?

Let us pray.

Almighty and everlasting God, who of your great mercy has gathered us into this fellowship, we search our souls in these moments to see how welcome Jesus would be with us in our walk through life. Let us resolve never to speak words or to condone actions that are not in accordance with the life and teachings of our Master, in whose name we pray. Amen.

At the Right Time

One of the great mysteries of the Second World War was the flight made by the German Rudolf Hess, a close associate of Hitler, to Scotland on May 10, 1941.

Many books have been published to explain this flight, and most of them convey the opinion that Hess carried a message from Hitler that he wanted to make peace with the British. Why? Because he intended to attack the Soviet Union, and he could not win a struggle against both opponents.

Why did Hitler not make his peace offer public? Because he believed that German morale would suffer a devastating blow if he did. So he sent Hess.

The whole truth may never be known. The story that was put out at the time was that Hess was insane or that he was trying to save himself. The Soviets have opened their files on Hess to journalists and scholars, but in Great Britain, the files remain secret. Exactly why they are still secret is not known. Nearly all of the leaders are dead. Hess himself died several years ago in a German prison.

History made clear that Great Britain was not ready to make peace with Hitler. Churchill and other leaders saw through his scheme. They knew that Hitler could never win a war against both Britain and the Soviet Union. So they did not respond to any proposal for peace Hess may have brought.

In history, timing is often seen later as more important than it seemed at the time. During one of the battles of the Civil War, the North could have forced the South to surrender if the North had followed up an attack. Often they waited for a day or two, and the chance slipped away.

In our Scripture reading for today, we learned that Jesus traveled to Galilee because he knew the Jewish authorities in

Jerusalem wanted to kill him. However, his brothers urged him to leave Galilee and go back to Judea, in order to win more followers there.

Jesus' response was that the right time had not yet come for him, so he stayed on in Galilee. This passage suggests that Jesus was following a particular plan. He knew that he intended to go back to Jerusalem at the time of the Passover, when thousands of people would be in the city. He believed that he would have a tremendous opportunity to offer his message to the people at that time.

Sometimes we do not give Jesus the credit for foreknowledge of his plans. He was not leaving everything to chance and luck; he knew exactly when he wanted to be in Jerusalem. The events of that final week of his life prove that he was right, even though the final result was his crucifixion.

In our affairs, also, timing is important. Often we do not reflect enough on exactly the best approach to make to someone we are trying to bring into our fellowship. Regrettably, we sometimes even argue with people in the effort to win them over, but disciples are made not by argument but by example. If we have an argument with someone over a religious conviction, we may feel that we have won the argument, but we will almost always lose the person.

We should, therefore, be aware of the time of readiness and of the action that is most useful to win other disciples to the way of Jesus.

Rudolf Hess's flight in 1941 gained nothing. The net result was that he would spend the rest of his life—almost fifty years—in prison. His (and Hitler's) estimate of British character was totally wrong, and his journey had the opposite effect from what he intended. It made the British even more determined to never give in.

Let us pray.

Almighty and everlasting God, who in a world of change promises us a vision of eternity, may we daily examine our attempts to bring disciples to Jesus, and may we be aware that more are won by love and compassion than by argument. And may we be sensitive to the readiness

91

of the moment, always available to speak the right word at the right time. We ask this in the name of Jesus. Amen.

READ FROM YOUR BIBLE: JOHN 14:6-14

Way—Truth—Life

A woman was driving along a county road on a summer afternoon. As she approached an old-fashioned iron bridge, she reflected on how many times her grandfather and her father had come down this road in a horse and buggy or a farm wagon.

She slowed as she approached the bridge, for ahead of her was a dump truck hauling materials to a new subdivision that encroached further and further into this rural environment.

The truck was almost to the opposite end of the bridge as the front wheels of her car touched the ancient bridge.

The next thing she knew, her car was in the creek bed and she was hanging by her seat belt. The bridge had collapsed, apparently just as the truck left it and as her car wheels touched it.

Luckily, the woman was not seriously hurt. Every year thousands of American bridges are nearer the point of collapse. In one state alone, more than five thousand bridges have been declared dangerous to the traffic that passes over them every day.

When we discovered how to build a bridge, an extraordinary leap forward was made. Prior to that time, streams had to be forded with great danger. In the winter, before bridges, few people were able to cross large bodies of water.

Today bridges are engineering marvels. In France a bridge still stands that was built more than 1,500 years ago. The drive from southern Florida to Key West is practically on a continuous bridge that stretches for 161 miles. Across Lake Ponchartrain near New Orleans, is a bridge 25 miles long.

The purpose of a bridge is to allow persons and goods to get to the other side of a river or gorge in safety. To feel that a bridge is unsafe and may collapse can cause enormous fear among those who must pass over it.

* * *
** ** **

In the devotional scripture for today, Jesus tried to bring to his disciples on their last evening together a word of assurance. The Jewish faith at the time of Jesus imposed high moral ideals on all Jews. These ideals were taught in the synagogues of the villages and towns, which most practicing Jews attended on the sabbath.

One particular value Jesus brought to the understanding of religion was that he made it more personal. The Jewish faith prohibited any image of God, but in Jesus people felt that they could "see" God. He is the way, or the bridge; he is the truth, the fundamental revelation of God; and he is the life—that is, God's channel and agent in the world.

Jesus' life and teachings are the standards by which we as Christians must live. It is not enough merely to "be good," for he has set up absolute ideals toward which we are to strive, such as the love of God and of neighbor.

In following his example, we in turn learn the ways he guides us as the way, the truth, and the life.

Let us pray.

To you, O Lord, we lift up our souls, our God in whom we trust, as we seek to discover the path, the integrity, and the existence of life as taught by Jesus. May we truly find in him the answer to our questions about the conduct of life every day, for he is our Savior and our Redeemer. We ask this in his name. Amen.

READ FROM YOUR BIBLE: II CORINTHIANS 5:6-15

Full of Courage

For most children, the death of a pet is the first experience of deep grief. How the child responds to this event depends on the child's emotional and intellectual development. Very young children have no concept of death. If a pet is buried, they may ask how the animal or bird will be able to see or eat underground. They should be told that the pet won't need to see or eat any longer.

Children in elementary school years has seen television productions that show death, but may not have experienced the reality in their own lives before. They are accustomed to seeing television stars reappear on other programs, so they may not immediately think that death is a permanent state. When a pet dies, they realize that all of life is not like television, and they may have some emotional moments. Parents should help to reassure them by letting them talk about the pet, even if it brings tears. The child grows stronger by dealing realistically with death at this age.

Teenagers may have a special problem with the death of a pet, particularly one that has been in the family for a long time. The teen years are a time of great stress, embarrassment, and uncertainty, and a teenager can talk to a pet about any matter that may be causing anxiety. If teens lose a pet, they may lose their closest confidant.

Children learn courage as they learn other aspects of life—by watching adults deal with crises. If adults seem solid and are able to cope, however imperfectly, with an issue like the death of a pet, the child will learn courage. Such courage doesn't mean that no tears are shed by the adult; crying does not have a bad effect on a child under such circumstances. The open expression of sadness will teach the child that life has its tragedies, but courage helps all of us to go on living.

When a pet dies, the child should not be told that it has been "put to sleep." Later, if a child has to go to the hospital for

As Christians, "we must always aim at those things that bring peace and that help strengthen one another" (Romans 14:19 GNB). Paul goes on to say in the portion we have heard today, "We who are strong in the faith ought to help the weak to carry their burdens. We should not please ourselves" (Romans 15:1 GNB).

If we live in this way, we follow the example of Christ. He never turned away from the opportunity to do good. His ministry was compressed into three years or less, so he must have often been tired. Yet, he never said to anyone, "I am too tired to help now."

To be concerned about ourselves is not in itself wrong, but if we are so wrapped up in ourselves that we cannot offer assistance to others, we are missing the point of being a Christian, according to the text we have heard today from the apostle Paul.

Often we shrink from going to the persons who need help the most. In such avoidance, we miss the opportunity not only to help someone else but to find the presence of God in our own lives.

Albert Schweitzer, who gave up careers as an organist and a theologian to go to medical school and become a medical missionary, taught that it is in the struggles we face that we learn who God really is. Therefore, if we do not struggle, especially if we try to avoid every struggle or every unpleasant experience, we are missing the opportunity for God to come to us with power.

Perhaps our lives would be enriched if each one of us could think of someone who needs our help and who would be surprised if we offered it. This person might be lonely, ill, or have some other great problem. Let us think at this moment of what we might do for that person and what the possible reaction may be.

Maybe such an experience would make Christ more real to us, too, for we are obligated to bear one another's burdens.

Let us pray.

Almighty and everlasting God, by whose tender mercy we are blessed day by day, we pray for the courage to help others bear their burdens.

Forgive us when we disdain the example of Jesus, whose thought always was of the needs of others. Pardon us when we think only of "me" and "mine" and "ours." We ask this in the name of the tireless Savior. Amen.

JUNE 27, 1993

READ FROM YOUR BIBLE: ROMANS 5:1-11

Getting Right with God

One of the worst evils of modern times, in the minds of many people, is the welfare system in this country. Yet, no one doubts that this system, with all of its shortcomings and defects, has made it possible for some deserving people to escape perpetual poverty.

A newspaper carried an account of Dorothy, who has been on and off welfare for seventeen years. She had several children of her own, and when her sister died, she took seven more into her home. Although the check she received for support seemed large, she ran out of food near the end of every month.

She has always been willing to work. Once, when her children were hungry and she had no food in the house, she went to a grocery store and asked for work so she wouldn't have to steal.

Through a unique program in the city where she lived, she had the opportunity to acquire training as a practical nurse. Today to support this large family, she works at jobs in two nursing homes.

What makes this program different is that it doesn't try to teach a person a new skill. It helps people to improve a skill they already have. For instance, if a person can type thirty words a minute—not enough to qualify as a typist in an office—she or he is trained to get up to sixty words a minute and is also taught to use a computer.

People who help train persons like Dorothy have found that one of their biggest problems is that these people have negative self-images. This attitude causes them to think they can never learn to be self-supporting. Before they can make progress, they must overcome this impression. Once they do, they can cultivate ways to inspire the confidence of others in them.

Dorothy believes that she is off welfare forever. The patients at the nursing homes where she works think she is the best. Some people would not want to work in a nursing home; they would rather be on welfare. But Dorothy has gotten right with herself, and now she has gotten right with other people who value her. And nine people have come off the welfare roll as a result of her determination and of the program that helped her.

* * *
** ** **

The text we have heard today is one of the clearest in the writings of Paul to explain the process by which one becomes right with God. Paul announces that it is not by works that one enters into the kingdom of God but by faith.

And what does "faith" mean to Paul? It begins with the hearing of the Word, and it ends in submission and obedience. Persons must hear the Word or message that is proclaimed to them through the New Testament, then they must finally make a total commitment to God. So faith for Paul means total commitment. This meaning suggests that mere intellectual assent is not enough to be called faith; faith involves the vital personal commitment of the whole person. We are free to accept or reject the call to faith.

The other aspect of faith for Paul is that it is completely given by God. That is, it is something offered to us, not something we can discover or earn.

When Dorothy made the decision to get off welfare, she did so because a means of "salvation" had been offered through retraining. She would likely never have been able to get right with herself until she decided that she alone could never achieve any level of self-support. Many people on welfare reject the opportunity that is offered; therefore, they never achieve the level of life that is possible for a person who can earn his or her own way in the world.

Salvation, according to Paul, works the same way. God, through Christ, has made the offer; we can reject it (or only mentally accept it, which is actually the same thing as rejection). If we accept this offer, the spirit of Christ is internalized in us, and we become new persons. This offer is what we call grace—the undeserved love of God.

It is a time for rejoicing.

Let us pray.

Almighty and everlasting God, who has proclaimed your eternal truth through the life and work of Jesus Christ, you know that sometimes we are not grateful for your offer of new life. We take your offer for granted, or we mistakenly think that intellectual assent is sufficient. For these attitudes, we beg your forgiveness, through Christ our Lord. Amen.

READ FROM YOUR BIBLE: I CORINTHIANS 3:10-23

Laying a Sure Foundation

After we get out of school, many of us forget some important lessons from history. From time to time, we need to be reminded of the values on which this nation was built.

In the earliest days after the Revolutionary War, efforts were made to establish a national government. The challenge was to divide the powers between a central government and state governments.

The party that favored a strong central government was called the Federalists. Alexander Hamilton was the leader of this group. The opposing party, called the Republicans at first and later the Democratic Republicans, was headed by Thomas Jefferson.

The Federalists were generally wealthy merchants or big landowners. The Jeffersonians drew their support mainly from Southern landowners, mechanics, and workers. The Federalists remained in national office through the administration of John Adams, but with the election of Jefferson himself to the presidency, the Federalist party began to lose strength.

The establishment of two major parties in the earliest years of the republic provided a basis for elected government that has continued on the national level since the early 1800s, though the parties and their names have changed considerably since those times.

In our time, we have seen the disasters that have befallen countries under the iron hand of communism. This political philosophy outlawed all dissenting parties. One of the miracles of recent years has been the decline of the communist party in Europe and the rise of opposition parties—a necessity if democracy is to flourish.

On this day of national celebration, we remember with thanksgiving those who laid such good foundations for our form of government in this country and for the freedom of choice that is basic to this freedom.

* * *
** ** **

Our text for today places emphasis on the necessity of a good foundation.

The Christian life has only one authentic foundation: Jesus Christ. Some people who are a part of the church have tried to build on other foundations: prestige, name dropping, life-style, snobbishness, and the like. The Christian life is inconsistent with such foundations, and, to further the analogy used by Paul in this passage, at the time of testing they will fail.

We may be at a loss as to why some people bother to become a part of the church when they so obviously do not wish to build on the foundation of Christ. We can only hope that these persons will in time, through their participation, see that their foundation must be reconstructed.

Though our passage emphasizes only the foundation, we must also keep in mind that the quality of the building to be erected on the foundation is also important. A magnificent foundation may have built upon it a structure that will not withstand the tempests of life. In a storm, a good foundation alone will not be a sufficient refuge.

The protection against these storms is a strong spiritual structure, which incorporates both a sound foundation (that is, knowledge of the saving work of Christ) and the building itself (that is, devotion to following the example of Jesus in doing good).

Now is the time for us to be laying our foundation and erecting the building of our spiritual existence.

In Europe one can see huge churches that have stood for hundreds of years. The churches are impressive, and beneath each one is a foundation that has stood the test of time.

Let us be certain that we are building on a sure foundation.

Let us pray.

Almighty God, all times are your seasons, and all occasions invite your tender mercies. On this day of national celebration, we give you thanks for your providence and care. As our great nation is based on the sure foundations of those who lived two hundred years ago, may we, too, bear well our responsibility to pass on these values to following generations. We ask this in the name of Christ. Amen.

READ FROM YOUR BIBLE: HEBREWS 10:19-25

Draw Near to God

In Japan there is growing a "religion" that is unlike any religion we know. It is called the Institute for Research in Human Happiness.

We usually think of citizens of Japan as people who are either solidly related to the ancient religions of that country or who are unrelated to any religion at all. This new religion, based on the search for human happiness, is the fastest growing sect in Japan.

It was founded only five years ago by a man who was formerly a finance officer at a major trading company. He has written more than a hundred books on his new religion. Persons who want to join are required to read ten of his books and then take exams on them. If they pass, they can move ahead to deeper spiritual levels, of which there are seven in all.

The success of his organization is confirmed by the fact that he has more than a million and a half followers. More than twenty-seven million copies of his books have been sold.

The religion is not easy to join. One highly educated man with an important position in a Japanese company reported that he quickly read the first book and took his test. To his amazement, he failed. A note suggested that he study harder and try again in three months.

When the founder had a birthday party, thousands of people crowded into a huge dome-shaped structure to celebrate with him. Those who could not get close enough to see him could watch on giant television screens.

Christian churches in Japan, in spite of their missionary efforts extending over many years, have only a million members. This new religion expects to have ten million members by the end of this decade.

* * *
** ** **

The Letter to the Hebrews was written to and for Jews who had become Christians earlier but who now were on the brink of giving up their faith. The purpose of the book was to show that Jesus, as the Son of God, was superior to the Old Testament prophets, even Moses; that he was superior to the priests in the Old Testament; and that Jesus, as our high priest, confers salvation on us.

The Old Testament taught that the system of animal sacrifices that took place at the temple was the way of salvation. The text for today declares that Jesus opened a new way to God through his own death. "So let us come near to God with a sincere heart and a sure faith," he says. "Let us hold on firmly to the hope we profess, because we can trust God to keep his promise. Let us be concerned for one another, to help one another to show love and to do good" (Hebrews 10:22-24 GNB).

Many kinds of religions offer themselves today: the television church of nationally known evangelists; the store-front church; evangelical tabernacles unrelated to any denomination; religions that teach that the purpose of religion is to bring wealth to those who donate to a particular cause; churches based on a particular personality. Some of these religions urge people to join for selfish reasons.

The Christian churches have never offered this kind of gospel of "me." They offer the gospel of Christ. It confers great benefits, but its appeal is not to selfishness but to service.

The new religion in Japan that was just described is built around the personality of one man. What will happen to that religion when this man retires? It will probably fall apart.

On the other hand, the Christian faith has been spreading and growing for almost twenty centuries. Its center is not a human personality but a divine-human person.

Let us also draw near to God with a sincere heart and a sure faith, holding fast to the hope we profess, because we can trust God to keep his promises.

Let us pray.

Almighty and everlasting God, father of all mercies, we draw near to you now in the moments of quiet devotion, that we may experience a sincere heart and a sure faith. Let us, too, show concern for one another, helping one another to show love and to do good. We ask this in the name of Jesus. Amen.

READ FROM YOUR BIBLE: I CORINTHIANS 9:6-15

The Priceless Gift

A movie came out a few years ago that told the story of a medical doctor who was working with patients ill with Parkinson's disease. Many of these people had spent all their adult lives in a hospital. For them time had stopped when they became ill, twenty or thirty years before.

The movie's plot was about how the physician, played by Robin Williams, helped one man, played by Robert DeNiro, become a functioning human being again through the use of experimental medicines. After taking the medication for a time, the man "woke up" from the life he had been living—a kind of stupor in which he scarcely knew where he was—and became normal, or almost normal.

The tragedy of the film was that after taking the medicine

for a while, the man relapsed into his former state when the medicine stopped working.

The effect that such a movie has on people is that it makes them realize how fortunate they are and how pitiful people are who suffer from such an illness. At the beginning there is hope as the person first awakens. As the individual seems to become more functional, confidence grows that this person will be released from the dungeon of mental and physical ailments. Then at the very moment when expectation is strongest, the affliction returns and hope is lost again.

After healthy persons see a movie or hear a story like that, they realize that they have so much to be thankful for, and that the measure of health they enjoy is a priceless gift.

* * *
** ** **

The text we have heard today is a part of a section in which Paul was reminding the people of Corinth of their responsibility to make a gift to the people in Judea. Our devotional reading continues with his reminder that the harvest is in proportion to the number of seeds that are planted. The planting of a few seeds will result in a smaller yield than the planting of many seeds.

The motive for such a gift should not be regret or a sense of duty but a sense of love. We are told that gifts we make not only meet the needs of the receiver but will also lead to thanksgiving to God. They will give glory to God because of the loyalty and generosity of those who offer such gifts.

The motive for such giving, of course, is one of gratitude. If we feel that we have received gifts, we are inclined to be more generous. Paul was reminding the Corinthians that they had already received a priceless gift through the gospel and that therefore they should be considerate toward the people in Judea.

Some of us have known the distress and suffering of ill health in ourselves or someone close to us. When we go through such an experience, we become aware of how so many people take for granted good health. We realize that good health is a priceless gift.

In the spiritual realm, we may be aware that we have received a priceless gift through Christ. No amount of wishing or good works will enable anyone to earn this gift. It is simply offered; we have the option of rejecting it, and, as we know, many persons do reject it. But to those who realize its value, it comes as a priceless gift.

Let us, therefore, show our generosity to others, not out of a sense of obligation or duty, but out of thanksgiving because we have received a gift we did not deserve.

Let us pray.

Almighty and everlasting God, give us grateful hearts for your priceless gift of Jesus Christ. Forgive us when we, in turn, give to others out of a sense of burden or obligation. We have received a gift that we did not deserve; let us in thanksgiving give to others out of the joy of receiving a gift ourselves. We ask this in the name of Jesus. Amen.

READ FROM YOUR BIBLE: I PETER 2:4-10

The Basis for Concord

Think for a moment of all the ties that bind people together: family, children, marriage, sports, hobbies, travel, job or profession, games, entertainment, church, service, to name only a few.

Two of these just-named activities—children and sports—often combine to bring neighbors and families into a closer relationship. But just the opposite happened in a town in New York.

There was one Little League team in the town. Some parents regarded the man who was in charge of it as too bossy, so they formed a separate league. The original league filed a lawsuit to stop the new team from calling itself by the name "Little League."

A reporter who investigated this story found that Little League baseball has many lawsuits pending. A player is suing because he was hurt when he climbed a fence to get a ball. A mother is suing another mother because they collided when the mothers were playing a ball game.

In one city, a coach fired a pistol at an umpire who had called one of his players out at home plate. In another, several adults were injured in a clash after a disputed call by the umpire. Another coach hit the father of one of the players after some sharp words were exchanged.

A psychologist, commenting on the strife, said that Little League baseball used to be a way for kids to have fun, but now in many communities it has become a battleground for adults.

* * *
** ** **

Our text for today calls upon every Christian to become a "living stone," to be used in the framing of a spiritual temple. The church, according to First Peter, is a "chosen race," a "holy nation, God's own people, chosen to proclaim the wonderful acts of God, who called you out of darkness into his own marvelous light " (I Peter 2:9-10 GNB).

The term *nation* here suggests a community of common values and goals, dedicated to establishing and maintaining a spiritual unity based on the common allegiance to Christ. In this unity, the ambitions of all individuals are subordinated to the good of the whole. Such a commitment avoids the strife that occurs when communities begin to fall apart over the unusual demands of one person or a minority.

Little League baseball ought to be committed to the enjoyment and growth of the youngsters who play. When adults interject themselves into what is essentially a game for boys and girls, what ought to be fun is turned into a battleground of adult egos. Such conflict produces a sorry example for our youth.

The church has witnessed similar disasters when one group is determined to overpower another by force of numbers or by caustic remarks. What happens then is that the pride of individuals obscures the purpose of the church and the sacrifice of Christ on which it is built.

Let us be mature in our decisions, thinking always of the one who is the head of the church. Let us proclaim the acts of God that have called us out of darkness, and find in the example of Christ the basis for our concord.

Let us pray.

Almighty and everlasting God, we pray for a new spirit in the church that will put away the excessive arrogance and pride that obstructs our sense of unity and community. May we see that the basis for harmony in the church and among God's people is the recognition that we are his temple and he is Lord of all. We make this prayer in his name. Amen.

The Guarantee

In a wealthy suburb of a large city, a man paid almost $700,000 for a house. Before the new owner moved in, he went back to inspect the house he had just bought.

This time, he took a closer look than he had taken when he was shown the house before the sale, and what he found at first shocked him and then made him furious. For one thing, he found that the "fog" that had appeared to cover the windows when he had looked at the house earlier was actually a residue that could not be removed. Then he found that the "gold" faucets in the bathrooms were not gold but brass. When he turned on the fountain on the front lawn, he found that the plumbing necessary to make it work was broken.

He called his attorney and filed a lawsuit against the seller, charging that she had deliberately hidden these defects from him. The courts agreed with the seller, however, underscoring the old rule of "let the buyer beware."

Some real estate brokers are working to introduce legislation in several states that will require the seller to sign a form that discloses all defects in a house that is put on the market. Several states already have such legislation, but it is not always effective. Sellers still may not disclose everything that is wrong with the house, hoping that prospective buyers will not notice them.

In one court case, the judge did not allow compensation to new buyers for a hole in the roof because he said the buyers could have found it if they had looked for it.

When people buy a new product, often a warranty or guarantee is included. The manufacturer stipulates the conditions under which the guarantee will be valid. For instance, a new car must be serviced at the intervals specified by the manufacturer. If that service is not carried out, the guarantee is void.

* * *
** ** **

Some people would like to have a guarantee in religion. In the early church, some leaders taught that any sins committed after a person was baptized would not be forgiven. For that reason, Emperor Constantine put off being baptized until he was on his deathbed. That was the nearest thing he could find to a guarantee of eternal life.

Does God offer us any guarantees? You might say that he does. The passage we have heard today spells out the design by which God has made it possible for us to be saved. It was God's pleasure and purpose from the beginning, says the letter, that we should be his children. This deliverance is a free gift from God, accomplished through Jesus Christ.

In today's marketplace, we never know when an appliance or a machine will work as it should. If it fails, however, we can go back to the manufacturer if we have not abused the item or used it unwisely, and we can expect free repairs or replacement.

Similar conditions prevail in our relationship with God. We are promised salvation through faith, but such faith must be more than mere verbal assent. It must be proven by our lives—our thoughts, our deeds, our devotion to the work of God in our world. Some people, unfortunately, seem to have the belief that once they are a part of the church they have an insurance policy against future disaster, no matter what they do thereafter.

Not so, according to the Scriptures. In order to maintain our relationship with God, we must follow through with integrity and sincerity. God is not fooled; if we are insincere or superficial, the guarantee is void.

If, however, we are faithful in all ways to our commitment, we shall not be losers.

Let us pray.

Almighty and everlasting God, grant us the gift of loyalty, that we may be true all our lives to the commitment we have made to you.

Forgive us when we cheapen the value of the sacrifice of Jesus by contradicting our pledge to be faithful disciples. We thank you especially for the integrity of your word, which is our guarantee. We ask this through Christ. Amen.

READ FROM YOUR BIBLE: HEBREWS 13:1-7

An Angel on Our Doorstep

Irving Berlin was a musical genius. Nearly everyone agrees on that point. What is not so widely known is that, reported in a recent biography, he became later in his life a cold, selfish man who trampled on the feelings of others.

Perhaps no song is better loved in this country than "God Bless America." It is our unofficial national anthem. Some of Berlin's other songs, like "Blue Skies" and "Easter Parade," are almost as popular today as they were when they were written forty or fifty years ago.

Irving Berlin's special talent seemed to be that he understood the moods of the average person, and he could set those moods to music.

Berlin was born and lived out his childhood in severe poverty. His parents were Russian immigrants who came to this country to start a new life. At fourteen years of age, Izzy Baline—that was his real name—left home to make his own living. He got his start in music as a singing waiter and as a singer in choruses of Broadway shows.

In 1911, he wrote his first hit song, "Alexander's Ragtime Band." He was only twenty-three years old. From ragtime music, he went on to write many other hit songs, and in the 1930s he went to Hollywood. Although he never learned to read music, he could pick out a tune, perfect it, then have someone else write the music.

By the 1950s, however, Irving Berlin was increasingly out of touch with the average American, and he became more and more absorbed in the business side of his fortune. When he died in 1989 at the age of 101, he was still one of this country's best-known and best-loved composers.

* * *
** ** **

Our devotional text for today begins with an emphasis on welcoming one another. One motive that is suggested for doing so is that an angel might be welcomed without our knowing it. (The image here is that an angel looks like any other person—no wings or other extraordinary appearance—as in the Old Testament. See Genesis 18.)

Unfortunately, we are living now in a society in which violence is common. We are much more cautious than were former generations about welcoming strangers into our homes. Even when we are willing to welcome strangers, the fear of violence hinders us.

But there are other times when we do not offer the hand of friendship. For instance, in some churches, visitors receive scant attention because the people who go there are smug and self-satisfied. They do not want anyone else to come into their "club." But the church is not a club; it belongs not to its members but to God. When we welcome people into our church, we are acting on God's behalf.

Irving Berlin's songwriting finally came to a halt because he lost touch with the feelings and dreams of the American people. These images and emotions had been the source of his talent. When he lost contact with this source by his obsession with the business side, his genius seemed to vanish.

In the church, as in other aspects of our lives, often the stranger or newcomer can bring new life and new skills into our fellowship. An angel is by definition a messenger from God. Failure to welcome the stranger may indeed prevent our receiving a message God has for us.

Therefore, we are advised by the text for today to welcome the stranger always, for who knows, this newcomer may have a special message to us from God himself.

Let us pray.

Almighty and everlasting God, the dwelling place of all generations, in this moment of reflection, we wonder whether we have ever turned away anyone who came as a stranger with a message from you for us. May we constantly be open to extending welcome to a newcomer who may be sent by you. We ask this in the name of Jesus. Amen.

AUGUST 15, 1993

READ FROM YOUR BIBLE: EPHESIANS 4:21-32

The New and True Life

How do you measure the passage of time? Here is one measure that many people use: Sixteen years ago tomorrow, August 16, 1977, Elvis Presley died.

For some people, this event was a partition of life into "time before Elvis died" and "time after Elvis died." Every year since 1977, on August 16, thousands of people go to Memphis on an annual pilgrimage. More than thirty thousand people go through his home, Graceland, during this week, and visit his grave in a garden next to the house. At about ten o'clock on the night of August 16, a candlelight procession will move from the street through the grounds to walk slowly past his grave.

Almost three hundred fan clubs still exist for this entertainer, called by his admirers "the King." Throughout the year, people come from all over the world to visit Graceland. On an average day, more than two thousand people will go through the house and grounds.

Perhaps more than any other people in the world, Americans are starstruck. We like to see the homes (and graves) of the stars of movies, television, or the stage.

From time to time, people report that Elvis Presley is still alive and is living under a different identity somewhere, but those who knew him best say that he was too proud of his image to ever live in obscurity. He could never, they say, assume a new life.

* * *
** ** **

Paul's Letter to the Ephesians has two main themes: the unity of the Christian community and the characteristics of the new life in Christ. The second theme is taken up in the middle of chapter 4, from which our reading for today comes.

We have perhaps become so "hardened"—maybe that is too strong a word, maybe "self-assured" is a better expression—to thinking about the Christian life that we cannot really feel for a person who has lived outside our religion. We are so accustomed to hearing the familiar terms of the gospel that it is no longer really "good news" for some—in fact, it is hardly news at all.

Paul was writing to people to whom the Christian faith was new, exciting, and challenging. We might use the metaphor of a young man meeting a young woman for the first time and each of them finding that there is something alluring in the other. They see faintly the prospects of great happiness if the relationship develops as they hope it will. Then imagine that this couple gets married. After many years, in all too many partnerships, the elements that made the union exciting in the earlier years now become taken for granted, or, in some extreme cases, these elements become a source of irritation.

Paul was writing to people who were still exploring the significance of becoming Christians. Then, as the Christian way was practiced more and more, they fell into some of their former ways. These practices Paul condemns in this letter.

For thousands of people around the world, Elvis Presley was a kind of savior, a religious figure. When he died, they couldn't believe it. Since his death, many of them have become inconsolable. But no human being is worthy of being an object of worship.

117

Paul told the Ephesians plainly that they must get rid of the old self, that hearts and minds must be made completely new, that the new life must be upright and holy. Later in our reading for today, Paul advises them to give up their feelings of bitterness, passion, insults, and all other hateful feelings.

This reading gives us some clues as to the substance of the new and true life. Our behavior is to be modeled after that of Jesus, who lived a life holy and upright, who showed no bitterness, passion, or any other hateful feeling.

Every human being has flaws, so no human can be our model. Only the Christ.

Let us pray.

Ever-living God, strengthen and sustain us with patience and understanding, that we may look closely to the life of the Savior as the model for the new and true life. May we, too, put away all hateful feelings and be kind, tender-hearted, forgiving one another as God has forgiven us. We ask this in the name of Christ. Amen.

AUGUST 22, 1993

READ FROM YOUR BIBLE: COLOSSIANS 3:12-17

Called to Peace

In a crowded store, a woman who is taking care of her grandchild for the day talks with a clerk as the child approaches a display of crystal goblets. With a quick motion, the child rakes the display off the table. After the expensive goblets crash to the floor, the woman says to the clerk, "She didn't mean any harm," then picks up the child and quickly leaves the department store without offering to pay for the damage caused by the youngster.

A retired man asked a friend to go with him to the opening of a new store selling golf equipment. When he drives to his friend's home to pick him up, he finds that man is keeping his grandson for the afternoon. The child is eating an ice cream cone. As they get into the man's new car, he is concerned, but his friend assures him that the little boy won't spill any ice cream. When they get to the store, he looks in the back seat, where the child was sitting alone, and sees a big ugly blob of melted ice cream on the upholstery. His friend sees it too, and dismisses it with the remark, "It will probably wash off easily."

A psychologist wrote an article saying that many children are being left at home to grow up practically alone as one or both parents work. In the evening, the parent (or parents) is too weary to confront the child about behavior problems, so the child assumes that his or her behavior is acceptable. Grandparents often do not intervene to correct the child, for the parents may resent such interference.

This lack of adult discipline is shown, according to this social scientist, in numerous ways by children and adolescents: the number of reckless young drivers on the road who show contempt for other drivers and do not hesitate to endanger the lives of others by disregarding posted speed limits; the rudeness they demonstrate to older people; the lack of manners, such as breaking into a waiting line at a restaurant or movie theater; malicious vandalism and graffiti in public places, such as the theft or destruction of street signs and the use of ink markers or spray paint to write profanity in public places.

Attempts to discipline children after acts of this kind do not always correct the problem and often lead to further alienation between the generations. Many parents would prefer to live with the problem than incur the hostility that will result if one tries to restrain the child. So youngsters may grow up with the notion that they can have their own way in society without regard to the feelings or rights of others.

The actions just described are one additional symptom that our society is badly fragmented. The disagreements between parents and children often do not end when their child leaves home, for the scars of bitter disputes linger on.

119

* * *
** ** **

The passage we have heard today suggests some characteristics that are needed badly in many families in this nation and elsewhere in the world: compassion, kindness, humility, gentleness, patience, tolerance. Far too many human relationships, both in the home and outside it, are heightened by the opposites of these, such as callousness, arrogance, harshness, impatience, and intolerance.

Regrettably, these marks are also found in the church sometimes.

Our reading for today says that "it is . . . [for] peace that God has called you together in the one body" (Colossians 3:15 GNB). This peace is a gift from Christ. Doing everything in the name of the Lord Jesus—that is, doing everything in his spirit and attitude—is the way to this peace, both in society and in our families.

Let us pray.

O God our Father, we pray for a new spirit in the world and in the church, that we may learn from Christ the way to improve lives in our homes as well as in our larger society. We pray that we may search for this gift of peace, which comes only from our Lord, in whose name we pray. Amen.

AUGUST 29, 1993

READ FROM YOUR BIBLE: I TIMOTHY 3:1-7

The Power of Self-control

On the television screen was a pitiful wreck of a man. He had once been one of the best professional athletes in the country.

Interviewed on TV, he described how he had used steroids, a medication, to increase his strength during the years he was a football player. Now he is suffering from a brain tumor that physicians think may be directly related to his use of steroids.

Today many college athletic teams have what they call a "weight coach." This man's responsibility is to help young athletes increase their strength in order to improve their performance on the playing field.

In the past, many of these coaches liberally gave steroids to players, and only years later have some found that they suffer irreparable damage to their bodies as a result.

Today, the use of these drugs is banned from the locker rooms of college and professional athletes. Today strength is taught the old-fashioned way: by lifting weights and other exercises that strength the bodies of the young without resorting to dangerous and artificial means. Also, athletes are no longer fed diets that contain a dangerously high level of fats; their diets today are controlled for the best present—*and* future—health of the young people.

One means of developing strength is through self-control. Many adults allow their bodies to lose strength by their failure to exercise or to eat a balanced diet. Health authorities warn adults that the patterns set in youth and childhood are likely to persist into the future. Tests have found that young people as young as eighteen already have an alarmingly high rate of physical problems brought on by the neglect of a healthful and balanced diet and proper exercise in earlier years.

These same attitudes apply to our spiritual lives as well. Good habits and strong discipline are required. A child, if left alone, would probably subsist on a diet of sweets. No parent would dream of allowing small children to choose their own diet. The maturity of experience by adults must control what children eat.

In a similar way, our spiritual life must not consist of merely the easy and tasty activities—that is, those that bring us

121

pleasure. The Scriptures do not teach that Jesus went around seeking a good time; he went around doing good. So he becomes the model for our behavior.

Such discipline requires that we study closely the attitudes of the Savior and that we imitate them as best we can in our own situation. For instance, he brought friendship and healing to many in his time who were considered outcasts, those who were ignored as being outside the mainstream of society. It is natural that we tend to want to associate with people like ourselves, but we must also look around for those who are outside our "circle" and find ways to help them.

No one ever said that being a Christian was going to be easy. As a matter of fact, Dietrich Bonhoeffer, a German theologian who was killed in the Second World War, warned against what he called "cheap grace"—that is, grace that was accepted freely without any intention of showing gratitude for it as evidenced by a changed life and the desire to reach out to others.

Young athletes find new strength through the natural development of their physical potential. The process is slow and often is not fun. But the attainment of a specific goal lies at the end of their labors if they persist.

We are offered the same promises. Let us, therefore, show a good example, so that no one may say a bad word about us and about the one whom we call the Lord.

Let us pray.

Almighty and everlasting God, giver of all good things, we pray today for new strength to live the Christian life according to your promises. Forgive us when we seek the easy or artificial way to enhance our style of life. Give us sincerity of purpose so that we may bring only honor to your name and that of our Savior, in whose name we pray. Amen.